THE MUSICIAN AS INTERPRETER

Studies of the Greater Philadelphia Philosophy Consortium

Michael Krausz, editor

Already published:

Joseph Margolis, Michael Krausz, and Richard Burian, eds.,
Rationality, Relativism, and the Human Sciences
(Martinus Nijhoff Publishers, 1986)

John Caputo and Mark Yount, eds.,
Foucault and the Critique of Institutions
(Penn State Press, 1993)

Joseph Margolis and Jacques Catudal, eds.,
The Quarrel Between Invariance and Flux:
A Guide for Philosophers and Other Players
(Penn State Press, 2001)

Michael Krausz, ed.,
Is There a Single Right Interpretation?
(Penn State Press, 2002)

Paul Thom

THE MUSICIAN
AS INTERPRETER

The Pennsylvania State University Press
University Park, Pennsylvania

Library of Congress Cataloging-in-Publication Data

Thom, Paul.
    The musician as interpreter / Paul Thom.
        p.   cm. — (Studies of the Greater Philadelphia Philosophy
Consortium)
    Includes bibliographical references (p.   ) and index.
    ISBN 978-0-271-03198-9 (cloth : alk. paper)
    1. Music—Interpretation (Phrasing, dynamics, etc.)—Philosophy
and aesthetics.   2. Music—Performance—Philosophy and aesthetics.
I. Title.

ML3853.T56   2007
781.46'117—dc22
2007026535

FOR *Cassandra*

Contents

Musical Examples

Acknowledgments

The book would not have reached its present state without the generous criticisms of Jerrold Levinson and an anonymous referee.

I would like to thank Jed Distler for his permission to reproduce part of his notational transcription of Art Tatum's *Elegy*. I also thank Boosey and Hawkes for their permission to reproduce parts of Stravinsky's *Variations (Aldous Huxley In Memoriam)*.

An earlier version of Chapter 4 appeared in my article "Toward a Broad Concept of Musical Interpretation," *Revue Internationale de Philosophie* 60, no. 238 (2006): 437–52.

Special thanks go to my research assistant Dr. Berenice Kerr and to the wonderful staff of Southern Cross University Library.

Introduction

> And then he sat down at the cottage piano and played us the whole composition out of his head, the first and the incredible second movement, shouting his comments into the midst of his playing and in order to make us conscious of the treatment demonstrating here and there in his enthusiasm by singing as well; altogether it made a spectacle partly entrancing, partly funny; and repeatedly greeted with merriment by his little audience. For as he had a very powerful attack and exaggerated the *forte,* he had to shriek extra loud to make what he said half-way intelligible and to sing with all the strength of his lungs to emphasize vocally what he played.[1]

The pianist portrayed in this passage from Thomas Mann's *Doctor Faustus* is doing two things at once. In playing the music, he is engaged in an act of performative interpretation. In speaking about the music, he is giving a critical interpretation of it. The object of interpretation is the same in both cases: it is Beethoven's Sonata in C Minor, op. 111. But there are two kinds—or two senses—of interpretation. The differences between them can be explained as follows. A performative interpretation is expressed in action; it *presents* the work in a certain light, and because of this, there is a sense in which the work is actually there, as part of the performer's action. By contrast, a critical interpretation is expressed in words; it *discusses* the work, and the object of critical interpretation may be absent. The comic juxtaposition of the two types of interpretation in this passage highlights the extent of their differences by showing that they get in each other's way.

This book is about musical interpretation. Musical interpretation contrasts

---

1. Thomas Mann, *Doctor Faustus: The Life of the German Composer Adrian Leverkühn as Told by a Friend,* trans. H. T. Lowe-Porter (New York: Penguin Books, 1968), 55.

with critical interpretation, but includes more than performative interpretation. An idea of what it includes can be gained by considering a remark of Alfred Brendel's in his essay on Liszt's piano playing.[2] Brendel says that Liszt did not teach his pupils how to play the piano; he concentrated on interpretation. What, then, did he actually teach them? Fundamentally, he must have taught them the art, rather than the technique, of playing the piano. This art of turning the score into a performance, however, presupposes a whole musical culture comprising a richly interrelated set of musical practices—or at least, it did presuppose such a musical culture in Liszt's day. Included in such a culture is an art of understanding what is explicit in the notation, an art of disambiguating and correcting it where necessary, of understanding what might be implicit in the notation but would have been assumed by the composer's contemporaries. This is the art of editing keyboard music, and it is part of the musical culture to which Liszt and his contemporaries belonged. It forms part of what I mean by musical interpretation. Liszt himself edited Bach's *Well-Tempered Clavier,* and among his pupils, Emil von Sauer edited Liszt's works, Karl Klindworth edited those of Chopin, Hans von Bülow edited Beethoven, and Alexander Siloti edited Tchaikovsky—to name just a few cases. Editing was not always a distinct activity from transcribing, as Brendel notes: "Every edition of older music, with the exception of those by editors like Bischoff and Kullak, was virtually a transcription. Bülow 'corrected' Beethoven. Adolf Ruthardt, with no qualifications as composer, virtuoso or musical thinker, turned every masterpiece he touched into an Augean stable."[3]

Related to the art of editing music, then, there is an art of transcription—in Liszt's case, the art of translating orchestral and vocal music into the language of the piano. This, too, is part of the musical culture in which Liszt flourished, and I include it under the rubric of musical interpretation. So, besides discussing performative interpretation, we shall also be considering those musical works that—like transcriptions, paraphrases, and variation sets—operate in a variety of ways on preexisting musical material. Liszt must have passed on some of his knowledge of the art of transcription and paraphrase, because among his pupils, Moritz Moszkowski penned transcriptions of Wagner, Moriz Rosenthal of Johann Strauss, Giovanni Sgambati of Gluck, Alexander Siloti of Ravel, Carl Tausig of Bach, and so on.

2. Alfred Brendel, "Liszt's Piano Playing," in *On Music: Collected Essays* (Chicago: A Cappella, 2001), 280.

3. Alfred Brendel, "Turning the Piano into an Orchestra," in *On Music,* 282–83.

Musical interpretation, therefore, exists at three distinct levels. At the editorial level, there is an art of deciphering musical scores, of contextualizing them historically, of adjusting and expanding them to make them suitable for performance. At the level of composition, there is an art of transcribing and adapting certain types of music to a form in which they reinterpret their originals in the language of the desired performative forces. At the level of performance, preexisting material is interpreted or reinterpreted through the local and global interpretations of performing artists. Franz Liszt was a master interpreter in all of these ways.

Liszt's mastery of the arts of editing, transcribing, and generally arranging music for the keyboard can be gathered from the following description.

> In 1844, at the height of Liszt's career as a pianist, a lover of Bach in Montpellier, Jules Laurens, reproached him with his charlatanry, and then asked him to play his famous arrangement for the piano of Bach's Prelude and Fugue in A Minor for organ:
> "How do you want me to play it?"
> "How? But . . . the way it ought to be played."
> "Here it is, to start with, as the author must have understood it, played it himself, or intended it to be played."
> And Liszt played. It was admirable, the perfection itself of the classical style exactly in conformity with the original.
> "Here it is a second time, as I feel it, with a slightly more picturesque movement, a more modern style and the effects demanded by an improved instrument." And it was, with these nuances, different . . . but no less admirable.
> "Finally, a third time, here it is the way I would play it for the public—to astonish, as a charlatan." And, lighting a cigar which passed at moments from between his lips to his fingers, executing with his ten fingers the part written for the organ pedals, and indulging in other *tours de force* and prestidigitation, he was prodigious, incredible, fabulous, and received gratefully with enthusiasm.[4]

Here we catch the great pianist reflecting on the interpreter's aims and acknowledging that they must be adapted to the intended audience. For one audience, the work is to be interpreted in the light of the composer's intentions; for another, the contemporary means of performance is paramount;

---

4. Charles Rosen, *The Romantic Generation* (London: Fontana, 1999), 510–11.

for a third, the work must be interpreted so as to entertain. Interpretation is not just interpretation-of and interpretation-by, but also interpretation-for.

The activities of editing music, transcribing it, varying it, and performing it may all have been embodied in the person of Franz Liszt, but that does not make them identical activities, and we should begin by clearly distinguishing them. I shall not have much to say about editing, because its differences from musical composition and performance are clear enough.

Transcriptions

To transcribe a musical work is to adapt it to a medium for which it was not originally devised. On the one hand, the transcription shares musical content with the original work; on the other, it reworks that content for a new musical medium. It follows that a transcription of a scored work must contain a different set of performance directives from those contained in the score of the original work. Therefore, if the identity of a musical work depends on what is prescribed in its score, a transcription is a different work from its original. This point is contested by Roger Scruton, who thinks that "the vocal score of an opera, in which the orchestral parts are transcribed for piano, is surely not another work."[5] Scruton argues that "the ruling intention of the transcriber is to preserve the pattern of pitched sounds as the composer intended it, but without the instrumental colour." He appears to assume that the instrumental color is not part of the work, and that may be a defensible view about a work's identity. The view I shall adopt, however, is that the identity of a work is determined by the set of determinative directives for performance in its score. On this view, scoring is part of the work's identity. The point is not a crucial one, though. As Scruton himself observes, "questions of identity do not ultimately matter."[6]

Of greater importance is the fact that what is foregrounded in a transcription is not its difference from the original material, but its sameness. That material may be presented in a new way, but the focus is on the material itself rather than on its reworking. Stephen Davies (writing about Brahms's transcription of the Bach Chaconne) points out that a performance of a transcription is not (thereby) a performance of the work transcribed, adding: "Of

5. Roger Scruton, *The Aesthetics of Music* (Oxford: Clarendon Press, 1997), 451.
6. Ibid., 452.

course, it is perfectly natural to say one hears Bach's Chaconne in Brahms's work transcription. Besides being natural, this is correct. The transcription would be a failure if it did not provide the auditor with epistemic access to (much of) Bach's work. But . . . a performance offering indirect acquaintance with one work need not be *of* that work."[7]

Obviously, the transcribing of a musical work is a different activity from that of rendering a performance into notation—which also goes by the name of transcription.[8] In both cases the output is a work for performance, but only in the former is the input such a work. Not so obviously, transcriptions differ from paraphrases. Paraphrases, like transcriptions, are of works rather than themes or styles. And like transcriptions, they adapt old content to a new medium. They differ from transcriptions in that they do not track the material's content bar by bar, but instead adopt a looser approach to it, taking bits from here and there in the material, mixing them up, and linking them by novel transitions that are not to be found anywhere in the material.

For Peter Kivy, performances are like arrangements.[9] It is true that both performances and arrangements can be called "versions" of their topic works, but we need to remember that performances are in other respects unlike transcriptions, in that their topic works are relatively abstract. There is also a distinction between work transcriptions and other types of musical arrangements, such as variations and homages—as Davies reminds us.[10] At first glance, it seems as if we could base these distinctions on the different types of object that variations, transcriptions, and homages have: variations are of themes, transcriptions of works, and homages are to composers (or to the composer's style). Up to a point, this idea works. Homages are indeed distinguished from transcriptions in the way claimed, and because of this a homage need not share any musical material with its object, other than the object's style. A transcription, by contrast, must share material with its topic

7. Stephen Davies, *Musical Works and Performances: A Philosophical Exploration* (Oxford: Clarendon Press, 2001), 179.

8. Ibid., 8 n. 2. For Davies, transcriptions are a type of musical *score,* but in common parlance they are a type of musical work. He does not consider this point, but he can accommodate it by treating the common usage as a secondary sense, derived from the primary one, by applying the name "transcription" to the *content* of what he calls transcriptions.

9. Peter Kivy, *Authenticities: Philosophical Reflections on Musical Performance* (Ithaca: Cornell University Press, 1995), 133–38.

10. Stephen Davies, "Transcription, Authenticity, and Performance," in *Themes in the Philosophy of Music* (Oxford: Oxford University Press, 2003), 49.

work in a much more specific way, usually by sharing all the principal melodic, harmonic, and rhythmic elements. Yet the distinction between transcriptions and variations cannot be reduced to the distinction between a work and a theme. A theme may be transcribed, as, for instance, when Brahms transcribes the "Saint Anthony Chorale" (along with its variations) for two pianos. Further, a work may become the subject of variations, as in Beethoven's variations for cello and piano on "God Save the King." The distinction between variations and transcriptions will be discussed in Chapters 1 and 2.

Variations

When we hear a variation as a variation, we are somehow cognizant of the theme as well. We hear the theme in the variation, in a way. The experience is perhaps like that described by Plato, the experience of intuiting the form in the particulars. The particulars strive after the form, or are approximations to it. The perception is of dependence, not just similarity. Malcolm Budd puts it like this: "A common form in music is that of theme and variations. Since an appreciation of a work of this form requires the listener to hear the variations *as* variations of the theme, the work can be said to be about the relational property of similarity in difference—the listener understands the work only if his experience of the music is imbued with this idea."[11] Similarity in difference can be experienced in two ways: as an experience of a type of sameness, or as an experience of a type of difference. The first type of experience is the more relevant to our experience of transcriptions, and the second, to our experience of variations.

We need to ask, however, whether something can *be* a variation even though we do not hear it as a variation. Willi Apel suggests as much when he says that "the meaning of the variation form lies in change," but change is one thing, and perceived change another.[12] On an objective understanding, what differentiates variations from transcriptions is the *relation* that binds them to their originals, regardless of whether this relation is perceived or not. A variation varies the content, while a transcription varies the medium. More precisely, a transcription varies the medium while not dis-

11. Malcolm Budd, *Values of Art: Pictures, Poetry, and Music* (London: Penguin Books, 1995), 170.

12. Willi Apel, *A History of Keyboard Music to 1700*, trans. and rev. Hans Tischler (Bloomington: Indiana University Press, 1972), 283.

turbing (so far as possible) the content, whereas a variation retains some parts of the content and varies other parts of it. The question of whether an objective account of this sort is adequate is addressed in Chapter 2.

Realizations

The performance instructions contained in a musical score explicitly or implicitly prescribe certain actions on the part of those who aim to comply with that score. They also explicitly or implicitly proscribe certain actions. And they leave certain actions open—neither prescribed nor proscribed.[13] I use the term "realization" to cover any way of narrowing the set of actions left open by such performance instructions, whether this is by way of performing the music in question or by annotating the score.

The art of realizing a piece of music includes an art of nuancing the score's dynamics and its other indications. As exercised during a performance, it involves a capacity to depart from a planned reading, adding decorations, flourishes, cadenzas, or other departures from the score. For instance, Liszt invented new ways of doing things at the keyboard, including a certain way of playing double chromatic scales that departed from the printed score. All this is *local* interpretation. At the level of *global* interpretation,[14] the musician-interpreter projects a vision of the work as a whole. Such a vision of the work may (or may not) be governed by a literary narrative. Liszt's circle, we know, made use of such narratives in interpreting the master's Sonata in B Minor as well as his Ballade in B Minor.[15] An awareness of these narratives in the audience no doubt helped the pianist project a global interpretation of the work.

Realizations should be distinguished from both transcriptions and variations. The essential difference lies in the fact that a realization includes its object, whereas a transcription or a variation does not. By this I mean that in order to play a realization of a piece of music, you have to do everything that is required in order to play that piece. By contrast, to play a variation

13. Paul Thom, *For an Audience: A Philosophy of the Performing Arts* (Philadelphia: Temple University Press, 1993), 77.

14. For this distinction, see Paul Thom, *Making Sense: A Theory of Interpretation* (Lanham, Md.: Rowman and Littlefield, 2000), 21ff.

15. Joseph Horowitz, *Arrau on Music and Performance* (Mineola, N.Y.: Dover, 1999), 137, 143.

on a theme, you have to do *different* things from the things you do in playing the theme. Similarly, to play a transcription of a piece you have to do
different things from what you do in playing the piece.

Stephen Davies thinks that while a performance of a work transcription
is not a performance of the work, a performance of an arrangement (such
as the Glenn Miller arrangement of "In the Mood") *is* also a performance
of the original song (authored by Joseph Garland and Andy Razaf).[16] Our
distinction between realizations and transcriptions gives us a way of explaining this difference. The reason is that the Glenn Miller is a realization of the
song, whereas a transcription is not a realization of its topic work. Any performance of Glenn Miller's version of "In the Mood" is also a performance
of the original song, because the performative actions specified by the Miller
arrangement *include* the performative actions specified by the song. The
same holds for any arrangement of the song that includes its melody line
and harmonies (and whatever other conditions it specifies). The relationship is one of realization. If you do the latter, you thereby do the former.
The same *cannot* be said for the Bach Chaconne for solo violin and a transcription of it for piano—or indeed of any case in which we are comparing
a transcription and its topic work. The identity of the Chaconne is not
exhausted by the notes on the page. If it were, then a piano transcription
that included all the original notes (along with a lot more) would stand to the
Bach work just as an arrangement of a song. The point is that Bach's piece
is not just a skeleton for a work—it is a work in itself, one that achieves a
remarkable fullness, partly by virtuosity, partly by suggestion. Essential to
Bach's achievement is the paucity of the means he uses. The work is not
constituted solely by its prescriptions for performance, but implicitly pro-
scribes certain actions. In declaring itself as a work for solo violin, it pro-
scribes filling out the harmonies on the keyboard. In general, a performance
of a transcription is not a performance of the original work, whereas a performance of a realization is also a performance of that which is being realized.

The succeeding chapters will discuss the arts of musical transcription,
variation, and realization, taking as our point of departure Ferruccio Busoni's
provocative ideas on these topics. In Chapter 1, we will critically examine
Busoni's twin theories that composition is a form of transcription and that
transcription aims to recover the composer's original inspiration. Busoni's
account of these matters will be contrasted, unfavorably, with the accounts
recently articulated by Stephen Davies, but I will propose some amend-

16. Davies, *Musical Works and Performances*, 180–81.

ments to what Davies says. In order to set this theory in an empirical context, we will discuss various actual keyboard transcriptions—literal, creative, and parodic—from the baroque and Romantic periods, as well as from 1940s jazz. We will examine the distinctions among paraphrases and other transcriptions.

In Chapter 2, we will test Busoni's ideas about the art of writing variations against a selection of examples drawn from Elizabethan, baroque, and late classical keyboard music and from jazz. We will also contrast his ideas with the remarkable ideas of Nelson Goodman on this topic. Strangely enough, both authors assimilate variations to the class of transcriptions; I will challenge this assimilation on several grounds. Variations foreground their differences with their material; transcriptions foreground their similarities with their material. A variation's subject can be distinguished from its theme, and because of this, it can represent its theme in ways that are not open to a transcription. Further, because variations come in sets, the members of which may refer to one another as well as to their common theme, a variation's reference to its theme may possess a level of complexity greater than what can occur in a transcription.

In Chapter 3, our discussions will center on the idea of a musical realization. Again, Busoni's theories will provide a convenient focus, and again we will find them wanting when compared with what Davies has to say on the topic. We will consider several examples of musical realization as recorded on piano roll, disc, and video. And in the last chapter, I shall attempt to draw the material together in a philosophical account of these interpretive activities. I shall reject a narrow conception of interpretation according to which interpretation is restricted to critical interpretation. A broad concept of interpretation takes transcription, variation, and realization to be different modes of musical interpretation linked by similarities of structure and purpose. I will show that these similarities are also shared by critical interpretations.

Notes on Representation and Meaning

Throughout the book, I will deploy two key concepts in ways that may not be congenial to some of my philosophical readers. These are the concepts of *representation* and *meaning*.

Representation is, at the least, a two-termed relation. A representation is a representation *of* an object (that which is represented) *by means of* a vehicle (that which represents). In a mathematical sense, one series of elements sometimes represents another series of elements: certain elements from one series can be mapped onto elements in the other, and there are functional relationships between certain features of one series and corresponding features of the other.[17] For example, the positive even numbers (series A) can be mapped on to the natural numbers (series B) as shown below.

| A: | 2 | 4 | 6 | 8 | 10 | ... |
| B: | 1 | 2 | 3 | 4 | 5 | ... |

Beyond this mapping of individual members of one series onto individual members of the other, there are relations connecting groups of elements in one series with groups of elements in the other. For example, the result of *dividing* two elements of series A is a function of the result of dividing the corresponding elements in series B, as 10/6 is a function of 5/3—namely, the former is equal to the latter. Again, the *sum* of two elements from series A is a function of the sum of the corresponding elements from series B, as 2+6 is a function of 1+3—namely, the former is twice the latter. These relationships hold by virtue of certain global features of series A. Because of the existence of these individual mappings and global relationships, series A can be said to *represent* series B.

Mathematical representations like this exist eternally and do not depend on human agency. Intentional representations, by contrast, come into existence as a result of human agency, and this difference needs to be taken into account when we think about such representations. Intentional representation is a three-term relation between a representing agent, an object, and a vehicle. Because there is a representing agent, those cases in which the agent presents the vehicle as representing the object can be distinguished from those in which the vehicle is a representation of the object, but it is not presented as such. Further, the object is an intentional object. It is not just a thing but a thing as construed by the agent. A drawing of a face, for example, is done by someone, and the face drawn is not just a face, but a face as construed by the artist. In general, a distinction can be drawn between an intentional representation's object and any model it may have. A model is something that the agent is emulating in the course of the act of representation. If there is a model in the case of transcriptions, variations, and realizations, it would be another transcription, variation, or realization. It would not be the musical work that is being transcribed, varied, or realized.

Intentional representation is different from mathematical representation, but sometimes it mimics mathematical representation as it aims to map the vehicle's aspects or elements onto those of the (intentional) object, in such a way that there are global relationships connecting certain of the vehicle's features with corresponding features of the object. Consider a drawing of a face. The drawing is the vehicle, and the object is a face (not necessarily any existing face). A drawing of a face not only shows the face's parts (eyes, ears, mouth, and so on), but shows various features of these elements (an expression such as a smile, for instance) in such a way that these features are functions of features of the corresponding parts of a real face.

Philosophers have articulated various specific concepts of intentional representation. Some philosophers speak of seeing or hearing the object *in* the vehicle.[18] Because this way of talking makes reference to what can be seen or heard in the vehicle, we have to ask, "Seen or heard by whom?" Evidently a representation of this type does not just have a vehicle, an object, and a representing agent; it also has an intended addressee in that it is *for* an intended audience, the members of which are intended to see or hear it in particular ways. The fulfillment of this intention is facilitated by suitable resemblances to the represented object, but it additionally depends on the existence of audiences who have learned appropriate ways of seeing and hearing that are acquired by immersion in the experience of relevant representational practices.

There is in this type of intentional representation a characteristic duality in our visual (and auditory) experience. Our attention is drawn now to the object, and now, consequently, to the vehicle, and vice versa. Roger Scruton speaks here of a "double intentionality":

> When I see a face in a picture, then, in the normal aesthetic context, I am not seeing a picture *and* a face; nor am I seeing a resemblance between the picture and a face. The face and the picture are fused in my perception: which is not to say that I confuse the one with the other, or mistake the reality of either. I am presented with two simultaneous objects of perception: the *real* picture, and the *imaginary* face. And my response to each is fused with my response to the other.[19]

18. Scruton, *The Aesthetics of Music*, 122, 125.
19. Ibid., 86–87.

I shall call this type of intentional representation *experiential* representation. Experiential representation is more specific than intentional representation, as we shall see in Chapter 2.

Representation in the arts is characteristically experiential. An experiential representation might still be what Arthur Danto calls a "mere representation," however.[20] An experiential representation's object, by definition, can be seen or heard *in* it, but that does not mean that the object is represented *as* anything in particular. A portrait of Napoleon could satisfy the definition of experiential representation, in that Napoleon can be seen in it, without its representing Napoleon *as a Roman emperor* or as anything else. To put it in terms favored by Danto, the representation might include no metaphorical transfiguration of its object.[21] The conception of an intentional representation that represents its object *as* something or other is important in relation to representational art, and I will refer to it as the concept of *aspectual* representation.

I am not assuming that aspectual representations are always experiential. That question will be broached in a later chapter. I am assuming that an aspectual representation applies what may be called a *treatment* to its object, in the sense that it is conceptually coherent. Not every intentional representation includes a treatment, because in some cases the relevant features of the vehicle do not cohere with one another. It may be that parts of the vehicle apply treatments to parts of the object, without the vehicle as a whole applying a treatment to the object.

Scruton favors an even more specific sense of "representation." He restricts representation to "the presentation of thoughts about a fictional world."[22] We might label this *fictional* representation. Scruton argues that music, because it does not present such thoughts, does not involve fictional representation. But of course that does not settle the question of whether music involves artistic representation. I shall be arguing that some musical phenomena do exhibit artistic representationality.

Meaning, like representation, is a concept that philosophers have defined in a multitude of different ways. Scruton makes a fundamental observation: "the meaning of music lies *within* it; it can be recovered only through an act of *musical* understanding."[23] Thus, to speak of musical meaning is

20. Arthur Danto, *The Transfiguration of the Commonplace: A Philosophy of Art* (Cambridge, Mass.: Harvard University Press, 1981), chap. 6.
21. Ibid., 167ff.
22. Scruton, *The Aesthetics of Music*, 127.
23. Ibid., 211.

not to commit oneself to thinking that music somehow denotes or refers to something beyond itself. (And yet, as we shall see, some music is meaningful by virtue of such a reference.) Scruton identifies a particular type of meaning—aesthetic meaning—in the following terms: "When a critic tells us that such and such is part of the meaning of a piece of music, then what he says can be accepted only if we can also experience the music as he describes it."[24]

Aesthetic understanding is the correlative of aesthetic meaning in Scruton's account: "If music has meaning, then that meaning must be understood by the one who understands the music. Hence the concept of musical understanding displaces that of musical meaning: we have no idea what musical meaning might be, until we have some grasp of the distinction between the one who hears with understanding and the one who merely hears."[25] The only rider I would add to Scruton's comments is that understanding, like representation, may be experiential or purely conceptual—and so, correspondingly, may musical meaning.

24. Ibid., 227.
25. Scruton, "Wittgenstein and the Understanding of Music," *The British Journal of Aesthetics* 44 (2004): 2.

Transcriptions

No one has written about the composition and performance of transcriptions and variations with a more unified vision, or more practical experience, than Ferruccio Busoni. His Bach transcriptions—especially the Chaconne for solo violin, the D Minor organ Toccata and Fugue, and the Chorale Preludes—are still in the concert repertoire. His theoretical works—*The Essence of Music* and *Sketch of a New Esthetic of Music*—have become classics. His piano playing is legendary. Busoni's theories have many facets, some relevant to work transcriptions, some to variations, and some to the realization of musical works. We shall discuss these different facets separately in this and the succeeding chapters.

An Idealist Account

In Busoni's time, his critics dismissed his transcriptions as of little musical value, and in his own defense he formulated a far-reaching notion of a transcription:

> The frequent antagonism which I have excited with "transcriptions," and the opposition to which an ofttimes irrational criticism

has provoked me, caused me to seek a clear understanding on this point. My final conclusion is this: Every notation is, in itself, the transcription of an abstract idea. The instant the pen seizes it, the idea loses its original form. The very intention to write down the idea, compels a choice of measure and key. The form, and the musical agency, which the composer must decide upon, still more closely define the way and the limits.[1]

To compose, then, is to "transcribe" an abstract idea, and this "transcription" is a realization of that idea, specifying details—such as the "measure and key" and "the musical agency"—that are absent in the abstract idea. In describing one activity as both transcription and realization, Busoni puts aside the ordinary concept of transcription. According to the ordinary concept of transcription, nothing can be both a transcription and a realization, because a transcription takes as its starting point a complete musical work that specifies one medium and substitutes the specification of a different medium, whereas a realization starts with an incomplete specification of a work and completes it by specifying details that are absent from the original. In the former case there is a process of substitution; in the latter, the process is one of augmentation. Busoni's concept of transcription, then, is an unorthodox one.

Busoni's talk of abstract ideas may suggest that he is committed to a Platonic ontology, but it is not really so. An ontological Platonist would have to believe that abstract musical ideas are discovered, not created, by composers, and that they precede that discovery. As I understand it, the abstract ideas that Busoni speaks of do not precede the composer's activity, and that activity is thought of as an act of creation, not discovery. The composer's abstract idea exists in the composer's mind, and Busoni is putting forward a psychological theory, not an ontological one, about the process of composition.

This, however, is not to deny that Busoni's theory shows signs of Platonic influence. Composition, he says, works by "inspiration" and occupies "free heights whence descended the Art itself."[2] These metaphors resemble those used by Plato in the *Ion,* where the rhapsode is seen as drawing inspiration

1. Ferruccio Busoni, *Sketch of a New Esthetic of Music,* trans. Theodore Baker (New York: G. Schirmer, 1911), repr. in *Three Classics in the Aesthetic of Music* (New York: Dover, 1962), 85.
2. Ibid., 84.

from a divine source.[3] Equally Platonic are Busoni's statement that the musical idea loses its original form as soon as it is given a physical embodiment and his metaphor of music "descending" from free heights. The intellectual context of Busoni's theory of composition is a psychologized Platonism—a musical idealism—according to which "music is primarily mental, and secondarily physical" and "musical ideas are more real than their physical embodiments."[4]

Someone with a predilection for realist over idealist ways of thinking will find difficulties with Busoni's claim that to compose is to notate a realization of an abstract idea. First, there is an epistemological difficulty: what evidence is there for the actual existence of these abstract ideas? In some cases of composition, there is such evidence—for instance, where the composer works from a sketch of the incipient work. If, however, there is no sketch, the postulated abstract idea will be entirely private, and in this case there will be no public means of checking the composer's notation against his idea, and no way of verifying Busoni's account.

Secondly, Busoni's account falsely assumes that the process of composition is goal-directed in a way that it generally is not. The model of the composer finding and then transcribing an abstract idea assumes that the process of composition has a predetermined, fixed goal. This simplistic view takes no account of the ways in which creative processes undergo changes of direction, sometimes as a result of events in the external environment, sometimes as a result of physical accidents that open up new possibilities for the emerging work. As Igor Stravinsky observed in his *Poetics of Music:* "The least accident holds [the composer's] interest and guides his operation. If his finger slips, he will notice it; on occasion, he may draw profit from something unforeseen that a momentary lapse reveals to him."[5]

Even if the composer (or any artist) begins with an abstract idea, the creative process is not simply one of notating, or otherwise implementing, that idea. If it were so, it would hardly deserve to be called creative. Creativity involves not just impressing form on matter, but also responding to unpredicted situations in the real world. These unexpected encounters may stimulate a creative response that could not have been predicted by an

3. Thom, *For an Audience,* 91–93.

4. Geoffrey Payzant, *Glenn Gould: Music and Mind* (Toronto: Key Porter Books, 1984), 80, 81.

5. Quoted in Eric Walter White, *Stravinsky: The Composer and His Works,* 2nd ed. (Berkeley and Los Angeles: University of California Press, 1979), 426.

inspection of the originating idea. To an idealist, creativity is a purely mental capacity, and the physical world can either be receptive to the impress of the artist's ideas or stand as an impediment to their implementation. To a realist, creativity certainly involves the mind, but it also involves the artist's inventive capacities in making something of unexpected physical realities.

Busoni adapts his general account of musical composition to the particular case of composing a transcription. He believes that the interpreter should strive to recover the composer's inspiration and the work's abstract idea: "What the composer's inspiration *necessarily* loses through notation, his interpreter should restore by his own. . . . it is the part of interpretation to raise it and reendow it with its primordial essence."[6] As Harold Schonberg put it (though less metaphysically), the interpreter should "bring out the Beethoven in Beethoven, the Liszt in Liszt, the Bach in Bach."[7] The idea that the musical interpreter returns to the composer's original inspiration may owe something to the Neoplatonic belief that "whatever derives from a higher principle will *resemble* it and will ultimately *return* to it."[8] At any rate, Busoni's account of transcription seems to be that the transcriber operates on the same abstract idea that inspired the composer, engaging in the same type of process as the composer, but making different choices from those that the composer made. The transcriber, like the composer, creates a realization of the abstract idea through a written score, but chooses a different "musical agency" from the one chosen by the composer for realizing this idea. Such is Busoni's account of transcription.

An objection suggests itself. If, as Busoni maintains, to notate a work is to transcribe an abstract idea, then every musical work is really a transcription, and the works that are ordinarily known as transcriptions are in reality transcriptions of transcriptions. A sharp-witted philosopher might think that this theory falls easy prey to a fatal objection. According to Busoni, the philosopher might say, to compose is already to transcribe; it follows, then, that what is composed—the musical work—is itself a transcription. Now, according to our ordinary conception, transcriptions are *of* musical works. So if all musical works *are* themselves transcriptions, then (assuming that nothing is a transcription of itself) there is an infinite regress of musical works, each a transcription of another—which is absurd.

6. Busoni, *Sketch of a New Esthetic*, 84.
7. Quoted by Ateş Orga and Nikolai Demidenko, liner notes to *Bach-Busoni Transcriptions*, Nikolai Demidenko, Hyperion CDA66566.
8. Thomas Mautner, ed., *The Penguin Dictionary of Philosophy*, rev. ed. (London: Penguin Books, 2000), 381.

But victory is not so easy. Our sharp-witted friend has *combined* Busoni's theory with the commonly used notion of a transcription, according to which all transcriptions are of musical works. This is unfair, because Busoni put forward his notion as an alternative to the commonly accepted conception of transcription. Busoni's notion of a transcription includes all musical works along with what are commonly called transcriptions. Given this distinction, Busoni can avoid the threat of an infinite regress if he sticks to his sense of the word "transcription," rather than the ordinary sense. In his sense of the word, some transcriptions are of musical works, and some are not; moreover, all transcriptions are also realizations. In the ordinary sense of the word, all transcriptions are of musical works, and no transcription is also a realization. The infinite regress of musical works arises only on the basis of two premises—first, that all transcriptions are of musical works, and second, that all musical works are transcriptions. In Busoni's sense, the first premise is false; in the ordinary sense, the second is false. So the threat of a regress vanishes.

Busoni's account of transcription may escape this criticism, but it faces others, including the difficulties that threaten his account of composition (as transcription is a form of composition). According to Busoni's account, to transcribe a musical work is to notate a realization of the same abstract idea that gave rise to the work, but to choose performance media other than those specified by the composer. Obviously this account, like that of composition, requires the existence of an abstract idea from which the process commences. Notice that the abstract idea in question is not primarily in the transcriber's mind. On Busoni's account, it comes from the composer's mind and is recovered by the transcriber in an act of interpretation. So the transcriber, if not working from a sketch by the original composer, is supposed to be working from an idea in the composer's head. As a generalization, this suggestion is just as implausible as the suggestion that the composer always works from an abstract idea. The truth is that transcribers, even though they have beliefs about the original composer's ideas, actually base their work not on the composer's ideas but on their own, and above all on really existing musical scores.

Consider Busoni's famous transcription of Bach's Chaconne in D Minor for unaccompanied violin ("arranged for concert performance on the piano").[9] Example 1.1 shows a passage from Bach's Chaconne; example 1.2

---

9. See Ferruccio Busoni, *Toccata and Fugue in D Minor, and Other Bach Transcriptions for Solo Piano* (New York: Dover, 1966), 69.

EXAMPLE 1.1 Johann Sebastian Bach, Chaconne in D Minor for unaccompanied violin

shows the corresponding passage from the Busoni transcription, illustrating the type of textures Busoni employed. Let us grant that Busoni was trying to recover Bach's original idea. Even so, we must remember that Busoni believed that Bach, in composing the Chaconne, derived his inspiration from the textures of the organ. Charles Hopkins makes the point: "Busoni's transcription emerges more as an adaptation of an original organ work than one for violin. Busoni did, in fact, take the view that the grandeur of Bach's conception was ill-suited to the violin and that its realisation in the transcribed form, which he had arrived at via, in effect, an internalised 'organ' version, more vividly conveyed the universality of the composer's vision."[10] One would have to say that if Busoni's transcription is bringing out the Bach in Bach, then the Bach brought out is not the historical Bach, but a Bach of Busoni's imaginings. In reality, he was working from Bach's score—even if his work was colored by his own notions about what Bach was doing.

If we are to follow Busoni's usage and understand a transcription as a realization of the original composer's abstract idea in different media from those specified by the composer, then we have to draw the conclusion that the Bach-Busoni Chaconne is not a transcription at all. The same conclusion will have to be drawn in relation to most, if not all, of the works that are commonly called transcriptions. If, on the other hand, our aim is to understand what a transcription is, in the ordinary sense of the word, then Busoni's account is of no help to us.

A Realist Account

In the ordinary sense of "transcription" (as opposed to Busoni's sense), the transcriber transcribes a mind-independent reality. Consequently, there is a public means of checking a transcription against what it transcribes. (Of

---

10. Charles Hopkins, liner notes to *Bach-Busoni Transcriptions—2*, Nikolai Demidenko, Hyperion CDA67324, 11–12.

EXAMPLE 1.2 Ferruccio Busoni, transcription of Chaconne in D Minor for piano

course, the work transcribed must have come into existence as a result of mental activity, but that is not to say that it depends on any such activity in order to remain in existence, once composed.)

The process of transcription not only operates on a reality but also produces one. The transcription that is produced, like the work on which it is based, has certain real features, and some of these will be found in the original work, while some will not. As indicated in the Introduction, the content of the transcription is the same as that of the original work, but the transcription differs from the original by presenting that content in a new medium. If the transcription is not performable in the new medium, it is like a directive that cannot be carried out. Such a directive would be unsuccessful, because it would not satisfy a preparatory condition that applies to all directives—namely, that it must be possible for the addressee to carry out what is directed.[11] Therefore, in order to be successful, a transcription must be performable in the medium that it specifies.

This is not a trivial requirement. There are published transcriptions that do not satisfy the condition of playability. Some are to be found in John Walsh's popular anthology *Handel's Sixty Overtures from All His Operas and Oratorios Set for the Harpsicord or Organ* (1750). Some of Walsh's transcriptions simply reproduce the pitches and rhythms from George Frideric Handel's orchestral originals, dumping these pitches and rhythms onto the harpsichord's two staves.[12] Walsh's transcription of the Overture to Handel's oratorio *Esther* will serve as an example (see examples 1.3 and 1.4 below). This transcription is not actually playable on the keyboard unless it is modified in certain ways. For instance, the player will have to ignore some of the right-hand ties.[13] Indeed, any keyboard transcription of the *Esther* Overture that preserves all the piece's pitches and rhythms will be unplayable—and if unplayable, then unsuccessful. Preservation of the pitches and rhythms, then, is not sufficient to ensure a transcription's success.

Nor is it necessary. Terence Best, in his edition of twenty of Handel's overtures in keyboard transcriptions by the composer himself,[14] has published a keyboard transcription of the *Esther* Overture that is markedly different from the Walsh version—and has argued that this is Handel's own transcription (see example 1.5). The differences between the two versions are striking. Handel's version is leaner than Walsh's, omitting most of the second violin part. The Handel transcription, then, does not preserve all the original pitches and rhythms. Yet it is a successful transcription, conveying the original's Italianate energy and elegance.

This, of course, is not to deny that a successful transcription *may* preserve the original pitches and rhythms. Some of Franz Liszt's transcriptions of the Beethoven symphonies provide spectacular examples. Liszt himself gave a self-deprecating account of these works in his preface to the published edition: "I will be satisfied if I stand on the level of the intelligent

11. John R. Searle and Daniel Vanderveken, *Foundations of Illocutionary Logic* (Cambridge: Cambridge University Press, 1985), 56.

12. George Frideric Handel, *Handel's Sixty Overtures from All His Operas and Oratorios Set for the Harpsicord or Organ* (London: I. Walsh, 1750), repr. as George Frideric Handel, *60 Handel Overtures Arranged for Solo Keyboard* (New York: Dover, 1993), 113.

13. These facts led Terence Best to describe this transcription as "incompetent." See George Frideric Handel, *Twenty Overtures in Authentic Keyboard Arrangements,* ed. Terence Best (London: Novello, 1985–86), 1:xiii.

14. Ibid.

| Oboe, Violin I |
| Violin II |
| Bassi |

EXAMPLE 1.3 George Frideric Handel, Overture to *Esther*

Andante

EXAMPLE 1.4 John Walsh, transcription of Overture to *Esther* for harpsichord

engraver, or the conscientious translator, who grasps the spirit of a work and thus contributes to our insight into the great masters and to our sense of the beautiful."[15]

Examples 1.6 and 1.7 give an idea of Liszt's practice as a transcriber of Beethoven. In his transcription of this passage, from the Scherzo of the Fifth Symphony, Liszt indicates the original instrumentation, thus demonstrating his concern with fidelity to his model. The fact that he succeeds in preserving all the original pitches and rhythms shows that same concern. Liszt also gives an alternative version playable on pianos with fewer than seven octaves, thus demonstrating his desire to adapt the music in a playable way to various new media.

If preservation of the original pitches and rhythms is neither necessary nor sufficient for a transcription's success, and part of that success consists of retaining the content of the original work, then we are left wondering what

15. Franz Liszt, *Beethoven Symphonies Nos. 1–5 Transcribed for Solo Piano* (Mineola, N.Y.: Dover, 1998), vii; translation by Alan Walker.

EXAMPLE 1.5 George Frideric Handel, transcription of Overture to *Esther* for harpsichord

EXAMPLE 1.6 Ludwig van Beethoven, Scherzo from Symphony no. 5

EXAMPLE 1.7   Franz Liszt, transcription of Scherzo for piano

is required in order for that content to be retained. The meaning of the preservation of content is not always clear. I believe that there is no absolute criterion on the basis of which we can give a uniform determination of what should be included in a work's content. The transcriber's decision about what to count as the work's content will be relative to his or her purpose.

In his article "Transcription, Authenticity, and Performance," Stephen Davies expresses the goal of transcription as "to reconcile the musical content of the original work with the limitations and advantages of a medium for which that content was not designed."[16] In the absence of an absolute criterion for determining content, I think we can say that the reconciliation of which Davies speaks comes to this: that in satisfying the requirements for a successful transcription, the transcriber must *find* a criterion for the preservation of the model's content that does not conflict with playability in the new medium. Walsh's failure to find a satisfactory reconciliation of transcription's two functions can be contrasted with Handel's success in doing so (by omitting some of the orchestral texture in a way that produced a convincing harpsichord piece conveying some of the original's sense) and with Liszt's success as well (even as he preserved all the original pitches and rhythms).

16. Davies, "Transcription, Authenticity, and Performance," 49.

The Intentionality of Transcription

The transcription and the original work, though realities, are also cultural products. Because of their status as cultural products, they are connected not only by relations of similarity and difference, such as might hold between pairs of naturally occurring things, but also by intentional relations that can hold only in a context of human design. The transcription is an intentional representation of the work. In standard cases, the transcriber presents it as such. Further, the transcriber creates the transcription after the fashion of a mathematical representation that maps the sequence of the work's temporal parts while reflecting certain global features of the original work.

The mapping of the original work's parts may be selective. Such is characteristically the case in those transcriptions that select a handful of tunes from an opera and weave them together in the form of a paraphrase or reminiscences. Of these, Charles Rosen observes: "The finest of the operatic fantasies . . . —*Norma, Les Huguenots,* and *Don Giovanni*— . . . juxtapose different parts of the opera in ways that bring out a new significance, while the original dramatic sense of the individual number and its place within the opera is never out of sight."[17] Rosen is talking about Liszt's treatment of his material. In the *Don Giovanni* paraphrase, for instance, Liszt represents different themes from the opera as being juxtaposed, thereby recalling their original meanings while suggesting new meanings, as in the passage (example 1.8) where he interweaves the "pathetic" figuration of the Overture with the Statue's warning phrases from the cemetery and the "Champagne Aria." The already sinister quality of the Statue's warning is heightened by its juxtaposition with the pathetic tones of the Overture; the Champagne Aria sounds more futile and hollow than ever when set over those tones from the Overture.[18] By these devices Liszt does indeed bring out a new significance (as Rosen puts it), and this significance is achieved not only on a conceptual level but experientially as well, as we hear the quoted fragments *in* Liszt's work.

Davies distinguishes a variety of purposes for which transcriptions are designed.[19] These purposes entail different ways of representing the original work. Some transcriptions are designed to facilitate rehearsal of a work

17. Rosen, *The Romantic Generation,* 528.
18. Ibid., 530–40. Rosen gives a detailed analysis of the semiotic effect of these combinations on the listener.
19. Davies, "Transcription, Authenticity, and Performance," 51–53.

EXAMPLE 1.8 Franz Liszt, paraphrase of Mozart's *Don Giovanni*

(e.g., piano scores of an orchestral ballet score). In such cases, the transcription is designed to represent the original work in an experiential sense. This must be so, because the rehearsing dancers are meant to hear the original score in the piano version. In fact, if this type of transcription is to represent the original work, the only requirement is that the work be recognizable in the transcription.

Other piano reductions have a different aim. Sometimes, these reductions serve a pedagogical purpose: they provide material on which students can practice their skills at orchestration. The students' activity is then governed by rules, and the constraints on what counts as a successful transcription depend on what those rules are. If the rule is simply that the students have to orchestrate the music without departing from the pitches and rhythms in the transcription, then the preservation of original pitches and rhythms is the only constraint on the way in which the transcription represents the original work. Davies points out that some transcriptions go beyond these pragmatic or pedagogical purposes and are designed to reflect upon the work transcribed, "enriching our understanding and appreciation of the merits (and demerits)" of that work.[20] Because reflecting on the original work entails representing it *as* something or other, transcriptions having these aims must function as aspectual representations.

20. Ibid.

Busoni's Bach Chaconne and Liszt's transcription of Beethoven's Fifth are, in their different ways, both experiential and aspectual representations of the works transcribed. An acculturated listener would have no difficulty in hearing the transcribed work in the transcription. A treatment is applied to the transcribed work, because it is not merely represented, but represented *as* something. What the object is represented *as* can be gleaned from our earlier discussion. The Busoni Bach Chaconne transforms Bach's slender sound structure into a grandiose edifice permeated by organ sonorities. The Liszt version of Beethoven's Fifth Symphony exudes the energy and heroism of Beethoven's original, and in addition (as a work for performance), Liszt's transcription exemplifies the idea of the pianist as hero as well as the idea of the hegemony of the piano. By the latter, I mean the attitude that Liszt expressed so clearly in his preface: "As a result of the vast development of its harmonic power, the piano is trying more and more to take possession of all orchestral compositions. Within the compass of its seven octaves it is capable, with but a few exceptions, of reproducing all the features, all the combinations, and all the configurations of the deepest musical creations. And it leaves to the orchestra no other advantages than those of contrasting tone colors and mass effects—immense advantages, to be sure."[21]

Every successful transcription represents its original. This representation must be experiential. The function of transcription is to maximize the recognizable preservation of the original work's features consistently with adaptation to the new medium. A transcription that could not be recognized as such would be a dysfunctional one. By contrast, it is possible for a successful transcription to offer no particular treatment of its model's contents. For instance, if we were to introduce minimal modifications into Walsh's *Esther* transcription to make it playable, it would be a successful transcription by virtue of having reconciled content and medium, but it would lack any particular treatment of Handel's orchestral material. It would not qualify as an aspectual representation.

Illumination and Transformation

Let us assume that we are dealing with a transcription that includes some treatment of the original work, or in other words, a transcription that rep-

21. Liszt, *Beethoven Symphonies*, vii.

resents the work aspectually. Two broad types can be distinguished. The aspectual representation may cohere with the original work's features and may support and strengthen the original work's aims, perhaps by illuminating the original work. In a second type, the aspectual representation may not cohere with all of the original work's features and may not support that work's aims; rather, it transforms the work in some significant way. Such a transformation may or may not be internally coherent, even if some of its features do not cohere with features of the original. A lack of internal coherence would indicate that the transformation had, in a certain sense, failed; nonetheless, this is a possible case and should be considered. On the other hand, if the transformation *is* internally coherent (but not fully coherent with the original work), then it may or may not be implicitly commenting on that work. If it does not offer such comment, the transformation simply supplants the original. If it does comment on the original work, then it may operate in such a way as to undermine that original, perhaps by parodying it.

Illumination

One transcription that casts new light on the work transcribed is Glenn Gould's piano version of Wagner's *Die Meistersinger* Prelude.[22] This is not a transcription for a pianist to perform publicly; rather, it was written specifically for the recording studio. Gould explains: "You can usually get through the first seven minutes without incident, and then you say, 'Okay, which themes are we leaving out tonight?'... For the record, I wrote a piano *primo* part for the last three minutes, recorded it, put on earphones, and then added whichever voice was missing as a piano *secondo*." Gould was clear that he wanted the work to be heard as a contrapuntal piece: "It's so contrapuntal that it plays itself."[23] As a result of Gould's novel scoring, the counterpoint is indeed audible to a far greater extent in the transcription than in the orchestral version. Arguably, Gould's transcription does not depart from Wagner's aims but supports them in such a way as to illuminate the work.

22. Glenn Gould, perf., *The Glenn Gould Edition: Wagner, Siegfried-Idyll, Wagner-Gould, Die Meistersinger von Nürnberg, Götterdämmerung, Siegfried-Idyll Piano Transcriptions*, Sony SMK 52650), track 2.

23. Quoted in Michael Stegemann, liner notes to *The Glenn Gould Edition*, 6.

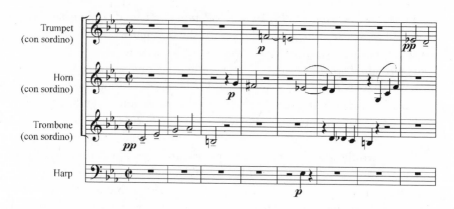

EXAMPLE 1.9 Anton Webern, transcription of the six-part Ricercar from
J. S. Bach's *Musical Offering* for brass and harp

Transformation

Roger Scruton reminds us that a transcription may have aesthetic properties quite divergent from those of the original work while retaining all the
original pitches and rhythms. He refers to Anton Webern's orchestration of
the six-part Ricercar from Bach's *Musical Offering* (example 1.9): "here
the orchestration compels you to hear Bach's melodic line as *background,*
the foreground being occupied by the short motifs which, for Webern, form
the true substance of this extraordinary work."[24] Scruton considers that
Webern's arrangement is not really a version of Bach's fugue at all,[25] but a
new work:

> the melodic line is broken into motifs, and stuttered out in timbres
> so opposed that the piece seems as though pulverized and reconsti-
> tuted out of tones that Bach would never have imagined. . . . It is as
> though Webern had set himself the task of composing anew the
> "Ricercar," from the sensibility of the serial composer, but arriving
> *at the very same notes* that Bach wrote. Not surprisingly, the result
> is not a version of Bach's great fugue, but another work—and a
> minor masterpiece.[26]

    24. Scruton, *The Aesthetics of Music,* 46. In treating Webern's orchestration as a transcrip-
tion, rather than a realization, I am assuming that Bach's original is scored for keyboard.
    25. Johann Sebastian Bach and Anton Webern, *Ricercar,* Münchener Kammerorchester
with the Hilliard Ensemble, Christoph Poppen, ECM New Series 1744 B0000048-02, track 1.
    26. Scruton, *The Aesthetics of Music,* 99–100.

Certainly the Webern is another work—but that is always true of a transcription. In calling it "not a version, but another work," Scruton draws attention to the fact that this transcription presents a highly distinctive treatment of its original. In a significant and coherent way it departs from Bach's aims and makes something new of the work. Nevertheless, it does not imply any (favorable or adverse) comment on Bach's work.

To me, the aesthetic coherence of Webern's treatment of Bach seems to be lacking in some of Leopold Godowsky's Bach transcriptions (see examples 1.10 and 1.11). In 1924, Godowsky published a number of transcriptions of selected Bach sonatas, partitas, and suites for either unaccompanied cello or unaccompanied violin. Listening to them, one is mightily impressed by the power of their pianism and the amazing, and at times off-putting, mixture of Bach's style with more recent traditions, as at the start of the Finale of the A Minor Sonata. Here, the cheeky bass line (particularly the *più piano* in the second bar) suggests something vaguely Russian and distinctly comic—qualities that have nothing to do with Bach's original and that sit uneasily with the remainder of Godowsky's transcription.

As we have seen, a transcription's lack of coherence with the original sometimes creates a new meaning possessing its own internal coherence, but not in this case. The effect, on this listener at least, is one of confusion. Bach's music can be heard in the transcription, but it is swamped by an alien setting that neither creates a new totality nor offers any comment on the original.

Another type of transformation is illustrated by jazz legend Art Tatum's 1940 version of Jules Massenet's "Élégie."[27] Brian Priestley notes that "Tatum's speciality...was to take a familiar melody, reharmonise it and decorate it with arpeggios and complex runs, sometimes in a *rubato* manner which was new in a jazz context and which made his in-tempo passages all the more effective. In this way the piece became a completely new experience, and two excellent if untypical examples are his versions of Massenet's 'Élégie' (which manages to incorporate a bizarre quotation from 'The Stars and Stripes forever') and of Dvořák's 'Humoreske.' "[28] The work that Tatum's *Elegy* transcribes is a song composed by Massenet for insertion into his incidental music for Leconte de Lisle's verse play *Les Érinnyes* (1873). Martin Cooper describes the song's mood as one of graceful nostalgia,

27. Art Tatum, perf., *The Definitive Art Tatum*, Blue Note 7243 5 40225 2 4, track 3.
28. Brian Priestley, "Ragtime, Blues, Jazz, and Popular Music," in *The Cambridge Companion to the Piano*, ed. David Rowland (Cambridge: Cambridge University Press, 1998), 218. Art Tatum, *Art Tatum: Jazz Masters,* arr. Jed Distler (New York: Amsco, 1986).

Allegro (Finale)

EXAMPLE 1.10 Johann Sebastian Bach, Finale of the Sonata in A Minor for unaccompanied violin

Allegro (Finale)

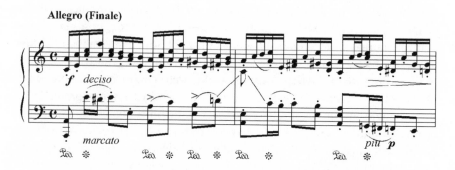

EXAMPLE 1.11 Leopold Godowsky, transcription of the Finale for piano

while noting that it seems "comically ill-assorted" with the savage material of the Greek tragedy into which Massenet inserted it.[29] The original song, with words by Louis Gallet,[30] can be seen in example 1.12. Tatum's arrangement, *Elegy,* replaces the nostalgic reverie of the original with a hectic right-hand vamp accompanying the melody in the bass (example 1.13).[31]

The lack of respect for Massenet's music is further heightened by the presence, in the midst of these variations, of quotations from "Souvenir" and "The Stars and Stripes Forever." What, asks a straight-faced Gunther Schuller, have these got to do with Massenet's "Élégie"?[32] Howard sees these interpolations as cadenza-like interludes,[33] taking the specific form of quodlibets, comparable to Bach's use of two popular tunes in the last of his

29. Martin Cooper, "Massenet," in *The New Grove Dictionary of Music and Musicians,* ed. Stanley Sadie (London: Macmillan, 1980), 11:801.

30. Jules Massenet, *Élégie* (London: Edwin Ashdown; Sydney: D. Davis, c. 1890).

31. Joseph A. Howard, "The Improvisational Techniques of Art Tatum" (Ph.D. diss., Case Western Reserve University, 1978), 2:147, measures the tempo as ♩ = 104.

32. Gunther Schuller, *The Swing Era: The Development of Jazz, 1930–1945* (New York: Oxford University Press, 1989), 485.

33. Howard, "Improvisational Techniques," 1:275–77.

EXAMPLE 1.12 Jules Massenet, "Élégie"

Goldberg Variations.[34] He refers to Donald Grout's definition of this type of musical quotation, which characterizes it as aiming to make "an incongruous and absurd mixture of texts."[35] The interpolation of these elements into the piece is not lacking in meaning (as Schuller's rhetorical question suggests). It simply underlines the comic intent of the whole piece—which indeed is obvious from its use of a drone bass with "The Stars and Stripes Forever." As if to underline the point, Tatum concludes with what sounds like a spoof on the closing series of chords in Rachmaninoff's C-sharp Minor Prelude.

In all these ways, Tatum's treatment of the Massenet song does not chime in with Massenet's aims, but clashes with them instead. Yet the effect is one of parody, not incoherence. In fact, Tatum's treatment of the Massenet song fits the pattern of parody as described by Margaret Rose: "parody in its broadest sense and application may be described as first

34. Ibid., 1:337ff.
35. Donald J. Grout, *A History of Western Music* (New York: W. W. Norton, 1973), 217.

Presto

EXAMPLE 1.13 Art Tatum's transcription of "Élégie" for jazz piano. Reproduced by permission of Jed Distler

imitating and then changing...another work."[36] According to Rose, the parodic nature of a work is signaled by the "comic incongruity between the original and its parody" and by "the changes made by the parodist to the original by the rewriting of the old text, or juxtaposition of it with the new text in which it is embedded." These descriptions neatly fit Tatum's *Elegy.* Rose goes on to identify a characteristic ambivalence of parody toward its object. On the one hand, "the imitation by the parodist of a chosen text has the purpose of mocking it and...the motivation in parodying it is contempt." On the other hand, "the parodist imitates a text in order to write in the style of that text and is motivated by sympathy with the imitated text."[37] One can perhaps hear the first of these motivations in the savage reversals to which Tatum subjects Massenet's song. The second motivation is detected by Ray Spencer, who speculates that Tatum's use of classical material was motivated by his desire to respond to those who thought that "the Negro was not clever or educated enough to tackle anything but jazz."[38]

The Cultural Value of Transcriptions

Deprived of Busoni's general argument for attaching high aesthetic value to transcriptions, can we find another way to articulate their value? Our account of the notion of transcription does not point to any uniform source of value, other than to say, with Scruton, that transcriptions play a role, or

36. Margaret Rose, *Parody: Ancient, Modern, and Post-Modern* (Cambridge: Cambridge University Press, 1993), 45.
37. Ibid., 45, 46.
38. Ray Spencer, "The Tatum Style," *Jazz Journal* (1966): 12. Quoted in Howard, "Improvisational Techniques," 1:354.

roles, in a musical culture.[39] But this statement needs elaboration, because the roles that transcriptions play in a musical culture are many and various, and (as we saw in the Introduction) "a musical culture" comprises, for example, music making, participating in living musical traditions, and exercising the craft of music.

The roles played by transcriptions in a musical culture can be articulated with reference to our conceptual frameworks of intentional, experiential, and aspectual representation—and of illumination, transformation, and parody, as against incoherent treatments. Davies's categorization of transcription types will also be useful. Music making takes many forms, and some of these make essential use of transcriptions (as a rehearsal aid, for instance—Davies's first type of transcription). Such transcriptions have to incorporate an experiential representation of the transcribed work, so that the work is recognizable in the transcription. But there is no need for the representation to be aspectual. Indeed, an aspectual representation, which gives the music an aspect that it lacks in its original form, could conflict with the transcription's purpose of building up in the dancers or singers a realistic expectation of what the music will sound like in performance.

Another type of music making that sometimes makes use of transcriptions takes place in households, at the hands of amateurs. Edward Said mentions these transcriptions in his book *Musical Elaborations:* "This practice argues the steady presence of amateur musicians who could not readily obtain or decipher full scores but whose desire to play the music could be satisfied by reading and playing it in piano versions."[40] Again we see the presupposition of an element in a musical culture, one that Roland Barthes calls "musica practica."[41] Eighteenth-century keyboard transcriptions of Handel's overtures provide an excellent example. These transcriptions had to incorporate an experiential representation of the transcribed work if they were to achieve their purpose of making the original accessible in the household. In addition, they could incorporate an aspectual representation of the music.

Living musical traditions are built up, in part, by repeated performance of individual works over time. More generally, they remain alive only through a continuity of cross-referencing within the tradition; indeed, the tradition can be seen as consisting of a web of such cross-references. Some

39. Scruton, *The Aesthetics of Music,* 455–56.
40. Edward Said, *Musical Elaborations* (London: Vintage, 1992), 5.
41. Barthes, "Musica Practica," in *Image-Music-Text: Essays Selected and Translated by Stephen Heath* (London: Fontana, 1977). Incidentally, Barthes held that this type of music making no longer exists.

of these cross-references are from one work to another, from transcription to original; these include the kind of illuminating, transforming, and parodying practices characteristic of successful transcriptions such as Gould's *Die Meistersinger* Prelude, Webern's Bach Ricercar, or Tatum's *Elegy*.

Another type of cross-referencing within a tradition occurs when a work refers not to another work, but to a practice. Said finds this kind of cross-referencing in the virtuoso piano transcriptions of composers such as Liszt: "The transcription for public concert purposes of operas, of music for other instruments (especially the organ) and for voice, as well as of full-scale orchestral works...makes a new kind of statement about the act of performance itself."[42] It is true that Liszt has emulated the faithful engraver in aiming for a high degree of accuracy in his Beethoven transcriptions. And it is true, as he himself says, that the transcriptions have an aesthetic aim. But talk of fidelity and beauty falls far short of capturing what is so daring about the ambition of these works and what is so stunning about their success. That ambition and success justify the claim that these transcriptions, in addition to illuminating or transforming the music they transcribe, also make a new kind of statement about the act of keyboard performance.

Liszt's transcriptions of Beethoven's symphonies fall, then, into Davies's fourth category (transcriptions designed to reflect upon the work transcribed). In this category we should also place Busoni's and Godowsky's Bach, along with Tatum's *Elegy*. One notable quality of transcriptions in the fourth category lies in the fact that they do not merely adapt the music to a new musical medium, but do so in a way that *exploits* the new medium's possibilities. Only by so doing can the transcription hope to attract attention to those possibilities, thereby making a statement about the medium.

There is a craft of music, and it embraces a multitude of skills, including the skill of orchestration. This skill is supposedly taught by the pedagogical use of transcriptions (piano reductions), as in Davies's second type of transcription. Such a practice presupposes that there is something to be learned about orchestration by this means. The transcription produced by the budding orchestrator can be regarded as an intentional representation of the piano score that formed its basis: it selects elements from the piano score, maps orchestral elements onto them, and applies a certain treatment.

The craft of music also includes the capacity to reconcile content and medium—a capacity that Davies regards as essential to transcription. This ability presupposes the existence of practitioners who have the judgment to

---

42. Said, *Musical Elaborations*, 6.

discern a musical work's content and also the practical knowledge of what is and what is not performable in a given medium. Earlier, we saw reason to think that Walsh (at least in his *Esther* transcription) was not fully adept at this craft.

Summary

According to Busoni's idealist account, transcription is a realization of the original composer's abstract idea. By this device Busoni hopes to persuade us that transcription possesses all the value that we attribute to original composition. In fact, transcriptions as such do not possess the value that we attribute to original musical compositions, composers do not usually work from an abstract idea, and transcription is not a type of realization.

The approach I have adopted is a realist one, but one that recognizes intentional relations and accordingly recognizes a difference between naturally occurring realities and realities that exist as a result of cultural production. The primary reality with which a transcriber works is a preexisting score. The minimal aims of transcription are twofold—to represent the work's content, and to do so in a new medium. Given these aims, a successful transcription must reconcile the aims of preserving the work's content and of writing a piece that is playable in the new medium. In order to do so, the transcriber must first determine what is to count as the original work's content. A transcription stands to its original work in a relation of intentional representation. The representation must be experiential, and it may or may not be aspectual. An aspectual transcription, if it is internally coherent, may illuminate, transform, or parody its work.

2

Variations

Busoni treats variations as similar to transcriptions, and this is understandable, because variation and transcription are two ways of arranging a model. If variation is a species of arrangement, however, then whatever is true of all arrangements applies to all variations. Using this general principle, Busoni argues that those musical literalists who deplore all arrangements while esteeming variations are involved in an inconsistency:

> Strangely enough, the Variation-Form is highly esteemed by the Worshippers of the Letter. This is singular; for the variation-form— when built up on a borrowed theme—produces a *whole series of "arrangements"* which, besides, are least respectful when most ingenious.
>
> So the arrangement is *not* good, because it *varies* the original; and the variation *is* good, although it "*arranges*" the original.[1]

Two different arguments jostle for attention here. On the one hand, there is an argument against the Worshippers of the Letter—those who

---

1. Busoni, *Sketch of a New Esthetic*, 86.

place the highest artistic value on original compositions as enshrined in musical scores. These people, it seems, esteem the variation form, because they regard variation writing as a form of original composition issuing in scores that demand respect. At the same time, they deplore variations as failing to respect the musical text that enshrines their theme. The argument concludes that the Worshippers of the Letter contradict themselves because on the one hand, they value variations as original compositions, but on the other hand, they devalue them for not respecting the letter of the theme. This argument is specifically directed against the Worshippers of the Letter, but it has nothing specifically to do with musical arrangements. There is also an argument against those who decry arrangements but esteem variations. These people—regardless of whether they are Worshippers of the Letter—contradict themselves, given that variations are a type of arrangement.

With regard to the first argument, it is true that anyone who condemns altering the text of a musical composition ought to think that this sin applies to the writing of variations, given that variations alter their theme. But are there such fanatics? Or are they simply an invention of Busoni's, contrived to give focus to a polemic? And with regard to the second argument, it is true that anyone who thinks that arrangements in general are an inferior breed of composition ought to think the same of variations, given that variations are a kind of arrangement. But the argument is *ad hominem*. It doesn't go to the heart of the question: what is a variation?

The relation between a variation and its theme is like that between a transcription and its original work in that a successful variation must be different from its theme, just as a successful transcription must be different from its original work. At the same time, we need to remember that transcription and variation, for all their similarities, are *different* ways of reworking a model. Transcriptions vary the model's medium, whereas variations vary its musical content.

The distinction between transcriptions and variations shows itself in a number of ways, none of which is acknowledged in Busoni's account. And the same defect is found in Nelson Goodman's account of variation, despite its superiority to Busoni's in most other respects.

Goodman's Account

In his article "Variations on Variation—or Picasso Back to Bach," Goodman takes the crucial relation between variation and theme to be one of reference. He claims that a variation refers to its theme by *exemplifying* certain features that they share and also certain features that they do not share.[2] Catherine Elgin puts his view succinctly: "A variation must be like its theme in some respects and different from it in others. But merely having shared and contrasting features is not enough. Otherwise, every passage would be a variation on every other. A passage does not qualify as a variation, Goodman contends, unless it refers to the theme via the exemplification of both sorts of features."[3] Regarding the exemplification of shared features, Malcolm Budd explains: "A work of art exemplifies a property if it both (literally) possesses and refers to it, as a sample both possesses and refers to whatever property it is a sample of."[4] Goodman adds that "to exemplify is to bring out, call attention to, but not necessarily to stress a feature."[5]

Goodman's account of variations is in one respect more determinate than Elgin's summary. He thinks that the variation exemplifies those features that it does *not* share with the theme in a metaphorical, not a literal, way. As an example of metaphorical exemplification, Elgin mentions Winston Churchill's exemplification of the attributes of a bulldog.[6] Goodman gives another example: "Consider for a moment how a giant can be called tiny. The term 'tiny' is here applied metaphorically to something that not this term but a contrasting term applies to literally. . . . Thus reference by a variation to a theme may be via a feature that literally belongs to one but only figuratively to the other. In this way metaphor is involved in *contrastive exemplification* and hence in variation."[7]

Now, if a feature is not shared by variation and theme but is possessed by only one of them, this leaves open two possibilities. Either the theme has the feature and the variation does not, or else the variation has the feature and the theme does not. Accordingly, if the variation-theme relation is to be defined in terms of the exemplification of shared features and the exemplification of contrasting features, then the definition could take one of two forms. We could define the variation-theme relation so that the putative variation exemplifies not only the features it shares with the putative

2. Nelson Goodman, "Variations on Variation—or Picasso Back to Bach," in *Reconceptions in Philosophy and Other Arts and Sciences,* by Nelson Goodman and Catherine Z. Elgin (London: Routledge, 1988), 72.

3. Catherine Z. Elgin, "Goodman, Nelson," in *A Companion to Aesthetics,* ed. David E. Cooper (Oxford: Blackwell, 1992), 176.

4. Budd, *Values of Art,* 169.

5. Goodman, "Variations on Variation," 69.

6. Elgin, "Goodman, Nelson," 175.

7. Goodman, "Variations on Variation," 71.

theme but also the features that it lacks but the putative theme possesses. Alternatively, we could define the relation as holding when the putative variation exemplifies features it shares with the putative theme and also exemplifies features that it possesses, but the putative theme lacks. Both definitions entail difficulties.

If we adopt the first definition, then the putative variation's exemplification of the contrasting features must be a metaphorical exemplification (as Goodman requires): a feature that is not actually possessed cannot be literally exemplified. Let us suppose, then, that we have two putative variations (V_1 and V_2) on a theme T, and that

> there is a set of features that both V_1 and V_2 share with T,
> both V_1 and V_2 literally exemplify the features in this set,
> T possesses another set of features, none of which is possessed by either V_1 or V_2, and
> both V_1 and V_2 metaphorically exemplify the features in this second set.

Under the proposed definition, this information is sufficient to show that both V_1 and V_2 are variations on T. And yet it might be that V_1 varies its theme in a different way from V_2. For example, V_1 and V_2 might apply different kinds of figuration to T. Therefore, even if the definition correctly identifies V_1 and V_2 as variations on T, it does not identify them as the variations that they are. They are the variations that they are by virtue of the features that they have in excess of the theme, not by virtue of the features that the theme has in excess of them.

So let us entertain the other definition of the variation-theme relation, and suppose that in order for one passage to count as a variation on a second passage, the putative variation must exemplify certain features shared with the putative theme and must also exemplify certain features possessed by it but not by the putative theme. (The exemplification in both instances may be literal—which is consistent with Elgin's version of the exemplification account, but not with Goodman's.) This definition meets our previous objection, because it picks up what is distinctive about each variation— what makes it the variation that it is—through the contrasting features, possessed by the variation but lacked by the theme. This definition faces another difficulty, however. A transcription, as well as a variation, may call attention to features that it shares with its model and may thereby exemplify those features; at the same time, it may call attention to features that it possesses but the model lacks, and may thereby exemplify those features. When all this happens, the transcription functions as a variation on the model, by Elgin's account. Useful as the account may be, it does not help us in distinguishing variations from transcriptions. At most, it provides an account of all arrangements, including transcriptions and variations. If we accept it as such, we still need a way of differentiating variations and transcriptions from one another. We will return to this question.

Theme

Variations are variations on a theme, and in a variation set, the theme is common to all variations, even if it is not everywhere explicit. This commonality can, I will argue, be satisfactorily picked up by our notion of representation—but not in any simple manner.

Initially, perhaps, one might think of a theme as a melody that is stated at the beginning and restated in each variation, but this would be an oversimplification. The theme may not be stated at the outset. In Igor Stravinsky's Concerto for Two Pianos, the theme of the *quattro variazioni* that make up the third movement is not stated until the fourth movement.[8]

Nor need the theme be a melody, though Stravinsky once thought so: "In writing variations my method is to remain faithful to the theme as a *melody*—never mind the rest! I regard the theme as a melodic skeleton and am very strict in exposing it in the variations."[9] Many variation sets do indeed have a melody as their theme, including the variations that make up the second movement of Beethoven's last piano Sonata, op. 111. The theme is an Arietta (example 2.1) whose serene, prayer-like melody will reappear, in an abstracted form, in the second (example 2.2) and succeeding variations in ever more foreshortened forms.[10]

Of course, Beethoven has a very singular way of making variations allude to their theme. Charles Rosen describes the procedure:

> How much of any given melody must be immanent in a variation, how much of the shape is essential, is largely a matter of stylistic definition. The whole of the theme is almost always completely

---

8. White, *Stravinsky*, 390–91.
9. Quoted in ibid., 309–10.
10. See Alfred Brendel, "Form and Psychology in Beethoven's Piano Sonatas," in *On Music*, 57.

Adagio molto semplice e cantabile

EXAMPLE 2.1 Ludwig van Beethoven, Arietta from Sonata no. 32 in C Minor, op. 111

recognizable in any of Mozart's or Haydn's variations. Beethoven, however, made the requirements absolutely minimal—only the barest skeleton of the melodic and harmonic shape is necessary, after which, of course, the superfluous elements of the theme can be used both dramatically and decoratively.[11]

The circled notes map onto elements of the original melody, tracking its progress, and this mapping (along with the reproduction of certain global features of the theme) makes the passage a representation of the original melody. The sequence of circled notes can be heard in the variation. This possibility makes the variation an experiential representation of the theme.

Yet a variation's theme does not have to be a melody. The *New Grove Dictionary* lists five other cases: *cantus firmus* variations, *ostinato* variations, fixed harmony variations, fantasia variations (that retain a melodic fragment or motif from the theme), and serial variations.[12] Let us consider some examples.

11. Charles Rosen, *The Classical Style: Haydn, Mozart, Beethoven* (London: Faber and Faber, 1971), 435.

12. Kurt von Fischer, "Variations," in *The New Grove Dictionary*, 19:537.

EXAMPLE 2.2 Ludwig van Beethoven, Variation 1 on the Arietta

Josquin des Prés's *Missa L'homme armé super voces musicales* uses the song "L'homme armé" as a *cantus firmus* with different settings in different movements of the Mass. Peter Phillips comments:

> the *L'homme armé* melody is quoted in turn on every note of the hexachord. This ascent starts on C in the *Kyrie,* proceeds to D in the *Gloria,* to E in the *Credo,* F in the *Sanctus* (given again, complete, in both Hosannas), G in the first *Agnus Dei* (incomplete) and A in the third *Agnus* (by which time it has at last become too high for the "tenors" to sing and has been transferred to the top part). The only sections to be completely free of the tune are "pleni sunt caeli" (*Gloria*), the *Benedictus* and the second *Agnus Dei.*[13]

Josquin's use of the *cantus firmus* involves an intentional representation whereby parts of the various movements map onto the song. A doubt arises, however, about whether all these settings involve experiential representation. Stephen Davies points out that in certain Renaissance Masses the *cantus firmus* cannot be perceived as such: "so long is the duration of each of the notes sung that the melodic fragment that is their source cannot be heard as such: rather than hearing a theme, one hears a succession of long, pitched notes."[14]

Consider now Bach's Goldberg Variations. The work's published title, *Aria with 30 Variations,* suggests that the variations are variations *on the Aria.* An aria is music that is sung, or, by extension, music in a singing style. Its essence is its melody. Thus, to call a piece of music an aria is to

13. Peter Phillips, liner notes to *Josquin: L'homme armé Masses,* The Tallis Scholars, Peter Phillips, Gimell CDGIM019, 3.

14. Stephen Davies, *Musical Meaning and Expression* (Ithaca: Cornell University Press, 1994), 358.

EXAMPLE 2.3 Johann Sebastian Bach, Aria from the Goldberg Variations

EXAMPLE 2.4 Johann Sebastian Bach, Variation 16 from the Goldberg Variations

draw attention to its melody. A naïve reader, encountering the title of this work and playing through the Aria, would expect the variations to include the Aria's melody in a varied form. That expectation, however, is dashed by the variations: their contact with the Aria is not with its melody but with its bass (circled in example 2.3).

What is essential to the Aria *qua* aria does not reappear, even in a varied form, in the variations. In fact, the variations are like a gigantic *ostinato* bass, a fixed bass line supporting a succession of different trebles. For example, in Variation 16 (example 2.4), the subject, elaborated in characteristic French roulades and dotted rhythms, forms the bass to a French overture.

The theme (the *ostinato* bass) is shown by the circled notes. The sequential mapping of these notes onto the theme makes this passage a representation of the theme. To be able to hear the theme in the variation is for the representation to function experientially. If the work's theme is what is common to all the variations, then the theme is not the Aria, but the Aria's bass line.

In serial variations, each variation is related to a given series of tones. For example, in Stravinsky's orchestral *Variations (Aldous Huxley In Memoriam)*, each variation is the inversion, or the retrograde, or the retrograde

EXAMPLE 2.5 Igor Stravinsky, series for *Variations (Aldous Huxley In Memoriam)*. Reproduced by permission of Boosey and Hawkes

EXAMPLE 2.6 Igor Stravinsky, retrograde of the same series. Reproduced by permission of Boosey and Hawkes

inversion of the series shown in example 2.5.[15] The first variation contains the retrograde, the second the retrograde inversion, and the third the inversion of this series (examples 2.6, 2.7, and 2.8), always in the same rhythm. Stravinsky himself emphasized the role of rhythm in these variations: "Some of us think that the role of rhythm is larger today than ever before, but however that may be, in the absence of harmonic modulation it must play a considerable part in the delineation of form. And more than ever before, the composer must be certain of building rhythmic unity into variety. In my *Variations*, tempo is a variable and pulsation a constant."[16] So of each variation it is true to say that it contains one of these alterations of the original series, while retaining a constant rhythm. In fact, the original series is never stated in the work, but there are *representations* of it in each of the variations. These representations map onto the series by standard musical operations of inversion and permutation, producing the original's retrograde.

It is doubtful, however, that the absent series can be *heard* in each of

15. White, *Stravinsky*, 535–36.
16. Quoted by White in ibid., 537.

EXAMPLE 2.7 Igor Stravinsky, retrograde inversion of the same series.
Reproduced by permission of Boosey and Hawkes

EXAMPLE 2.8 Igor Stravinsky, inversion of the same series. Reproduced by
permission of Boosey and Hawkes

Stravinsky's variations. If it cannot be heard, then we have to say that each
variation represents the original series intentionally, but not experientially.
On this point, it may be well to recall Stravinsky's remark about the difficulty
of this piece: "The question of length (duration) is inseparable from that of
depth and/or height (content). But whether full, partly full, or empty, the
musical statements of the *Variations* are concise, I prefer to think, rather
than short. They are, whatever one thinks, a radical contrast to the prolix
manner of speech of our concert life: and there lies the difficulty, mine with
you no less than yours with me."[17] Stravinsky shows that the theme may
be nowhere explicit in a variation set. It may be implicit in the way that a
series is implicit in its inversion and retrograde inversion.

Further puzzles about the notion of a theme emerge from a consideration
of William Byrd's keyboard variations named after the popular song "The
Woods So Wild." In Elizabethan variation sets such as this, the successive
presentations of the theme are numbered from 1 onwards, there being no
"null" presentation of the theme *sans* variation. This practice suggests that
we are to take the first presentation (see example 2.9) both as the statement
of the theme and as its first variation. But how can that be? Is the first variation a variation on itself?

17. Quoted in Joan Peyser, *To Boulez and Beyond: Music in Europe Since "The Rite of
Spring"* (New York: Billboard Books, 1999), 114.

EXAMPLE 2.9 William Byrd, "The Woods So Wild," no. 1

An alternative would be to say that the theme is the song tune, and the variations, including no. 1, are variations on it. That would mean that Variation no. 1 was both a setting of the theme and a variation on it. A setting of a tune, however, is not a variation on it. To set a tune is to take a relatively abstract piece of music—consisting solely of a melody, or a melody and harmony—and fill in some of the detail that it lacks (for example, a bass line and some counterpoint). A setting is thus a realization of its model. A variation is not a realization. Goodman notes that despite the similarities between the performance-work and variation-theme relations, "the several performances of a work are *not* variations" on it.[18] And, we may add, what applies to performances applies equally to all realizations, including settings.

Can we then say that the theme is the song tune, and all the variations *except no. 1* are variations on the song tune? One problem with this definition is that some of the variations do not contain the song tune or even anything recognizably derived from the tune. In fact, Byrd's variations on "The Woods So Wild" differ from the Goldberg Variations in not having a single element that runs through all variations. Some variations, such as no. 4, lack the melody (example 2.10). Others, such as no. 2, change the

18. Goodman, "Variations on Variation," 67. Goodman thinks that a work's performances *constitute* the work, but we need not agree with him on that.

EXAMPLE 2.10 William Byrd, "The Woods So Wild," no. 4

bass (example 2.11). Finally, some variations lack the harmony. For instance, on the third dotted minim of bar 1, Variation no. 4 lacks the sixth harmony.

In order to extricate ourselves from this puzzle, we can say that the tune's first presentation is a setting of it, and that this setting is the theme of the variations. Each variation in Byrd's set has something in common with this theme, though there is nothing that the theme has in common with all variations. The theme is, however, represented in each variation, because each variation includes a set of elements (different sets in different variations) that map onto elements in the theme.

Subject and Representation

The concept of a theme, as just outlined, is not sufficiently fine-grained to capture the specific links that bind a variation to its theme, given that these links may change from one variation to another. Accordingly, we need to distinguish between a variation's theme and its subject. By the subject, I mean those of the theme's elements that link a variation with its theme. From one variation to another, the theme is constant, but the subject might vary (if different variations retain different sets of the theme's features). The composer chooses a subject at each variation, and by virtue of the subject, the variation functions as a representation of the theme. The theme is bound to be multifaceted, and different facets may be chosen as the subject for each succeeding variation.

EXAMPLE 2.11 William Byrd, "The Woods So Wild," no. 2

In the Beethoven variations (op. 111) and in the Goldbergs, each variation has the same subject—the original melody and the bass line, respectively. In the Stravinsky *Variations,* the inversion, the retrograde, and the retrograde inversion of the original series are successively chosen as the subject. In the Byrd variations, too, individual variations relate to their theme in multiple ways. Different aspects of the theme are chosen successively as the variations' subjects. No. 2, the first variation (example 2.11), has a subject that includes the theme's melody, bass, and harmony. The jaunty motif that forms the subject of no. 4 (example 2.10) derives from a phrase of a rising third that occurs in bar 2 (treble) and bar 3 (bass) of the theme (example 2.9). No. 9 retains only the theme's harmony (example 2.12). The subject of no. 12 (example 2.13) includes both the rising-third motif and the theme's melody, which does not enter until halfway through the variation, and then only in the tenor voice. What was the start of the theme is now given a delayed entry.

In all cases, the theme is represented in the variation by means of mappings from elements in the vehicle (the variation) onto elements in the object (the theme). This representation is achieved via the variation's subject. So, if the subject is only a part of the theme, the representation will take the form of synecdoche.

Representation is not the same as presence. The variation represents its theme, but that does not mean that the theme is present in the variation. The variation's subject may include only part of the theme, or (as in the Stravinsky *Variations*) it may represent the theme without including any of

EXAMPLE 2.12 William Byrd, "The Woods So Wild," no. 9

it. Nor does the representation of the theme by the variation entail that the variation is somehow present in the theme, as some authors seem to think. Edward Said, for example, thinks that all thirty Goldberg variations are already implicit in their theme, "as if the gigantic work is somehow secreted within the theme in fragile outline."[19] Said's thought derives, perhaps, from Donald Tovey's comments: "As the [reprise of the] Aria gathers up its rhythms into the broad passage . . . with which it ends, we realize that beneath its slight exterior the great qualities of the variations lie concealed, but living and awake; and in the moment that we realize this the work is over." These remarks suffer a merciless riposte at the hands of Lawrence Kramer:

> The return of the aria is literal, and its literalness suggests something more boxy than organic. Its neat, perhaps overanxious orderliness can be taken to pose the question of whether the theme is the true source of the mighty design or merely the pretext for a musical abundance that may or may not be contained by that design, or any other. The design itself, driven by a series of canons, is conspicuous, even pedantic. But in what sense does the aria contain a canon in embryo, let alone a whole canonic matrix, let alone the other variations placed within the matrix? Does a mass of traces

19. Said, *Musical Elaborations,* 24.

EXAMPLE 2.13 William Byrd, "The Woods So Wild," no. 12

from the aria, or rather from its bass line, really constitute a relationship of coming-from?[20]

Kramer asks whether the relationship between Bach's theme and his variations is like that of organic generation, of a living being to its true maternal source, or whether it is something more prosaic, overly orderly, pedantic, "boxy," a mere pretext for creating something that is merely "a mass of traces" of its theme. This is a false contrast. Of course the theme is not simply a pretext for the variations, but is rigorously connected with each one of them. At the same time, Tovey's position is flawed. The relationship between theme and variation is not that of womb to offspring. The variation is a possibility within the theme, not in the biological sense that is paradigmatic for an Aristotelian concept of potentiality, but in the weaker logical sense that it is compatible with the theme. As Kramer points out, this weaker sense does not carry any implication of organic generation.

Goodman observes that "a variation on a theme . . . may be a variation on other themes."[21] In other words, it sometimes happens that a variation has more than one subject. This occurs with *variation pairs*. Willi Apel notes

20. Lawrence Kramer, *Musical Meaning: Toward a Critical History* (Berkeley and Los Angeles: University of California Press, 2002), 262–63.
21. Goodman, "Variations on Variation," 67.

EXAMPLE 2.14 William Byrd, "The Woods So Wild," no. 5

the presence of such pairs in Byrd: "The ordering principle of the variation pair, which still plays an important role in Mozart, Beethoven, and Brahms, is probably employed for the first time by Byrd, e.g., in *The Woods so wilde*."[22] Numbers 4 and 5 of Byrd's "The Woods So Wild" form such a pair. In no. 5, the first half of the rising-third motif that formed no. 4's subject is extended into a rising-scale figure (see example 2.14).

The second variation of the pair can be seen as a variation not only on the theme, but also on the first member. This ambiguity creates a dual subject. Considering no. 5 in relation to the theme, the subject includes the theme's bass line—along with scattered occurrences of both the theme's melody in diminution (boxed in example 2.14) and the rising-third figure from the theme (circled in example 2.14). Considered in relation to no. 4 (example 2.10), no. 5 retains the rising-third motif and supplies a different ending. Thus, in relation to no. 4, no. 5's subject consists simply of the rising-third motif.

What is true of variation pairs is true, by extension, of sequences (such as the rising pitches in Josquin's *L'homme armé*, or the rhythmic foreshortenings in Beethoven's op. 111) in which each variation stands in the same relation to its immediate predecessor. The existence of variation pairs and sequences shows that a variation can have two subjects, both relating to a single theme.

22. Apel, *History of Keyboard Music*, 283.

Variations differ from transcriptions in not needing to maximize the extent of their dependence on the features of the original (in this case, the theme). In the Beethoven variations, only the general shape of the original melody is preserved in the variations. In the Stravinsky, though the variations do preserve certain abstract features of the theme, they do not do so in an audible way. We can, therefore, distinguish among those variations that represent their theme and those that provide an experiential representation of it. No parallel distinction exists in the case of transcriptions. The point of transcription (to make the original work's content accessible in a new medium) would not be served if the transcription did not offer an experiential representation of the original. But the theme may not be audible in its variations. Its constant audibility is not always valued; in fact, where the theme is constantly audible, we tend to think of variations as routine or formulaic.

Treatment

The variation form highlights difference. In Spanish music, variations are called *diferencias*. The difference between a variation and its theme may not be implemented in a coherent fashion, but if it is, then the variation constitutes a treatment of the theme. A treatment may illuminate the theme, or it may transform it in a variety of possible ways.

Arguably—at least, according to some critics—incoherence occurs in the third variation of Beethoven's op. 111 (see example 2.15). In this variation, a new statement of the theme bursts upon us with unexpected force and redoubled energy. Certain critics hear this level of energy as not consistent with the general character of the movement. Joseph Horowitz appears to express this view in an interview with Claudio Arrau:

> JH: The third variation is quite violent. Is it perhaps closer to the struggles of the first movement than to the exaltation of the second?
>
> CA: No, no, no. The type of assertion is completely different. It's like looking back at life before leaving it. It is a joyful assertion of life on earth. I find it wonderful, the way it emerges a last time, this attachment to life.[23]

23. Horowitz, *Arrau on Music,* 164.

EXAMPLE 2.15 Ludwig van Beethoven, Variation 3 on the Arietta, op. 111

In Horowitz's view, but not in Arrau's, the third variation seems like an ill-fitting outburst in the context of the variation sequence. Now, given that each of the op. 111 variations draws its character from its place in the sequence (because of the progressive rhythmic foreshortenings), one might argue that a lack of coherence with the other members of the sequence amounts to a lack of internal coherence.

Sometimes the treatment illuminates the theme. In Byrd's Variation no. 2 (example 2.11), a shift in register up an octave suffuses the theme with light: it is as if, in our walk through the woods, we had suddenly stepped into a clearing. (In one manuscript, these variations are titled "Mr birds wandringe the woodes.")[24] At other times, the treatment metaphorically transfigures the theme, and in certain cases verbal labels exist for these trans-figurations. In many of the Goldberg variations, the treatment draws on familiar musical forms—not only the canon but also the gigue, the French

24. Davitt Moroney, liner notes to *William Byrd: The Complete Keyboard Music*, Davitt Moroney, Hyperion CDA 66551/7, 72.

EXAMPLE 2.16 Johann Sebastian Bach, Variation 20 from the Goldberg Variations

overture, and the *pièce croisée* (where the player's hands, one on each keyboard, cross each other). Thus in Variation 20, the subject is there as always, but it is split between the two hands (as shown by the circled notes in example 2.16). Bach has turned an aria into a *pièce croisée,* just as elsewhere he has transformed it into a canon, a gigue, or a French overture.

In other cases, no words capture the transformation. Beethoven's variations in op. 111 can be heard as so many settings of the theme. This possibility makes them aspectual representations. True, the variations are unlike the representation of Napoleon as a Roman emperor, in that there is no label by means of which we can say what the theme is represented *as.* But that is simply because Beethoven's setting is unique. He, like Napoleon's portraitist, has clad his subject in transformative garb.

As with transcriptions, variations may treat their objects (their themes) in ways that imply either positive or negative attitudes toward them. The range of these possible attitudes is summed up with wit and percipience by Alfred Brendel in an essay on Beethoven's Diabelli Variations: "The theme has ceased to reign over its unruly offspring. Rather, the variations decide what the theme may have to offer them. Instead of being confirmed, adorned and glorified, it is improved, parodied, ridiculed, disclaimed, transfigured, mourned, stamped out and finally uplifted."[25] Brendel explicitly describes some of the variations as "parodying" the theme,[26] and he identifies a number of techniques that Beethoven uses to this end—including the deformation of the theme's highly regular phrase lengths.[27]

25. Alfred Brendel, "Beethoven's Diabelli Variations," in *On Music,* 114.
26. Ibid., 126.
27. Ibid., 115–17.

Representation and Reference

Our account has been based on the relation of representation, but Goodman denies that representation is a necessary condition of variation:

> a variation on a representational painting may be purely abstract, representing neither the painting nor its subject nor anything else. Conversely, a picture of a painting—for example, a picture showing the painting as seen from the back or the edge—is not always a variation on it. Even a picture that represents both the painting and its subject—for example, a slavish copy—need not be a variation on it. In sum, representation is neither a necessary nor a sufficient condition for variation.[28]

He is contrasting the representational with the abstract—but this is not the sense of "representation" that we have been using. In our sense, an abstract painting can represent various things, and it can do so experientially or aspectually. Goodman himself clearly has this concept, even though he does not use the word "representation" for it. For example, he uses the following expressions in describing one of Picasso's variations on Velasquez's *Las Meninas:* "The solicitous maid, painted with Van Gogh–like urgency, becomes an agitated, threatening figure."[29] The variation in question is abstract, yet it contains elements that can be recognized as referring to one of the maids in *Las Meninas* under the aspects implied in Goodman's description. So, I take it—using this more generic concept of representation—that for something to function as a variation, it must represent its theme.

Goodman bases his account of variations on the relation of reference—in particular, the relation of reference by exemplification, which he cashes out in terms of bringing out or calling attention to the exemplified features.[30] By contrast, our discussions thus far have been based on a relation of representation. Is there a way of translating a reference-based account into a representation-based account? I shall argue that there is, given some intuitive assumptions.

First of all, we must remember that the notion of reference employed by Goodman is a rather thin one, certainly not as rich as the notion of refer-

28. Goodman, "Variations on Variation," 75.
29. Ibid., 80–81. The Picasso works are reproduced between pp. 82 and 83.
30. Ibid., 69.

ence that is implicit in describing a variation as making a comment on its theme. Second, we need to make a slight modification to the Goodman/Elgin account. That account, reduced to its essentials, says that a variation calls attention to the fact that it has a certain set of features (when, in fact, the theme also has them). It also calls attention to the fact that it has a second set of features (which the theme does not have). Now, strictly speaking, this formulation is insufficient to capture what a variation calls attention to. If we leave aside the purely hypothetical case in which a passage is, in fact, a variation on a certain theme, but is not presented as such, then we will want it to be the case not only that the variation agrees with the theme in certain respects and contrasts with it in others, but also that it *presents* itself in both these lights. In other words, we will need to say that what the variation calls attention to is the fact that it shares a certain set of features with the theme (not just to the fact that it has those features), and that it draws attention to the fact that it has a second set of features that are not shared by the theme (not just to the fact that it has those features). With this modification, the reference-based account postulates, for each variation of a theme,

> a set of features shared between variation and theme,
> a way of calling attention to the fact that the variation has these features,
> a second set of features possessed by the variation but not by the theme, and
> a way of calling attention to the fact that the variation has these features.

On a representation-based account, assuming that we are talking about variations that present a treatment of their theme, we postulate that the variation represents the theme and that this variation is aspectual. The reference-based description implies the representation-based description. If a putative variation and theme are related as described by the reference-based account, then the putative variation does indeed represent the putative theme, because there will be a mapping from it to the theme (obtainable from the first set of features), and it will present the theme under a certain aspect (implied by the second set of features).

The reverse implication does not hold, however. If the variation represents the theme, it may have two sets of features related as above. But the existence of these relations of similarity and dissimilarity is not necessary.

Representation may be achieved not by reproducing some of the object's features, but by establishing a functional relationship (other than identity) between some of the variation's features and some of the theme's features. We need to invoke a concept of functional dependence if we want to account even for very simple cases of mathematical representation. (See, for example, the mapping of two series in the Introduction.) And in the realm of intentional representation, if we are to do justice to variations such as the Stravinsky set, we need to be able to say that a variation's features are functionally related to those of the theme. I therefore believe that the representation-based account is more general than—and thus superior to—the reference-based account.

Summary

To Busoni, and also to Goodman, variations are essentially the same as transcriptions. Busoni treats both as simply a type of arrangement subject to the principle that he applies to arrangements in general. Busoni's principle is a principle of *sameness*. The transcription (or the arrangement in general) aims at identity with the composer's inspiration. By contrast, as have seen, the principle that governs variations is a principle of *difference*. Unlike Busoni, Goodman acknowledges the importance of difference in variations. His account articulates a referential structure that binds a variation by relations of difference and sameness to its theme. Like Busoni, however, he fails to articulate what makes variations different from transcriptions.

Variations are indeed like transcriptions in a number of ways. Both are intentional representations of an object. In both cases, a set of features is shared by the representation and the object, and there is a presentation of the fact that this set of features exists. If we leave aside cases that apply no treatment, we can say that transcriptions and variations also resemble one another by virtue of a second set of features possessed by the representation but not shared by the object—and by virtue of the presentation of the fact that this second set of features exists. In both cases, where a treatment exists, it may illuminate what is already present in the theme. It may also make something new of the theme, or effectively comment on it by placing it in a positive or a negative light.

Yet variations differ from transcriptions in a number of respects. First, as Stravinsky's *Variations* demonstrates, a variation's theme, unlike a transcription's topic work, need not be immediately recognizable. Accordingly, whereas a transcription has to represent its object experientially, a variation does not. Second, there is the distinction between the theme and the subject of any individual variation—a distinction not found in transcriptions. Third, as we saw in Byrd's variation pairs, a variation may have more than one subject, whereas a transcription has a single parent work. Fourth, variations usually come in sets, so that within a single work a theme has many variations. Even though a work may have many transcriptions, these transcriptions do not occur within a single work. This introduces a difference of a higher order: not only is each variation different from its theme, but successive variations also introduce *different* differences from the theme. These must all be compatible with their theme, but that does not imply that they are potentially present in the theme. Fifth, where a transcription's parent work is never part of the transcription, the theme of a variation set is sometimes part of the individual variations (as in Beethoven's op. 111) and sometimes not (as in Stravinsky's *Variations*).

Finally, the principal difference between a transcription and a variation lies in their manner of presenting the features they share, or do not share, with their objects. A transcription highlights the shared features, and a variation highlights the unshared features. Consequently, a single work might be counted indifferently as a transcription and a variation, depending on what kind of presentation of those features we impute to it. For example, if we take Godowsky's versions of Bach's solo string music as highlighting the features that they share with Bach's originals, then we will understand them as transcriptions. If we take them as highlighting the features that are not shared with the Bach originals, then we will understand them as variations.

Realizations

By a realization of a work for performance, I understand any way of making more determinate its performance directives. There are two means by which we could bring about a realization of a musical work. We could annotate the score, making its indeterminate directives more determinate, or we could execute the piece. Realizations are thus either notational or executive. The distinction is analogous to the distinction drawn by theater theorists between a production and a performance of that production.[1]

Notational Realizations

Notational realizations are what Roger Scruton calls versions: "Performances are not versions; but versions are made for performance, and they reflect the need to descend from the abstract particular which is the work of music to the concrete event which is its realization, through intermediate steps which may themselves involve a creative act, an imaginative meditation

1. David Saltz, "What Theatrical Performance Is (Not): The Interpretation Fallacy," *Journal of Aesthetics and Art Criticism* 59 (2001): 305.

on the original as the composer defined it."[2] A notational realization could include markings such as bowings, breathings, and fingerings. It could include other markings, such as phrasings, tempo indications, dynamics, and other expression marks. It could include written-out cadenzas and ornaments. It could also include alterations to the score such as thickened chords, descants, counterpoints, or additional orchestration.

A setting of a tune (such as Byrd's setting of "The Woods So Wild") counts as a realization of it on this account. So does a quotation of a piece in the course of a larger work (such as Brahms's quotation of "Gaudeamus igitur" at the end of his *Academic Festival Overture,* or Stravinsky's quotation of the Schubert *Marche Militaire* in the course of his *Circus Polka*). Thus notational realizations fall into two broad types, depending on whether they are intended as musical compositions or merely as preparatory steps in planning a performance.

The application of this simple scheme to real cases is not always straightforward. An interesting example is Stravinsky's 1941 orchestration of "The Star-Spangled Banner."[3] Those familiar with the American national anthem had no difficulty recognizing it in Stravinsky's version. Those familiar with Stravinsky's music might have been hard put to recognize him as the arranger. While Stravinsky reharmonizes the familiar tune at a couple of points, he does not inject much of his own style into it. All the more surprising, then, to hear that the work was later censured on the ground that it defaced the original: "after Stravinsky conducted it with the Boston Symphony in 1944, the police informed the composer of a Massachusetts law against tampering with national property, and removed the parts from Symphony Hall."[4]

What explains the reaction of the Boston authorities? That "The Star-Spangled Banner" should be regarded as national property is not so extraordinary. That Stravinsky should be accused of tampering with it is more intriguing, because the accusation implies that he made changes where he should not have. The authorities must have regarded Stravinsky's work as a setting of the familiar tune, but one that did not preserve the original content in the way it should have. Therefore, they must have regarded that content as including not just the melody but also the usual harmonies. Apparently Stravinsky did not share this view of what was essential to the

2. Scruton, *The Aesthetics of Music,* 454.
3. Michael Tilson Thomas, cond., *Stravinsky in America,* London Symphony Orchestra, RCA 09026-68865-2, track 1.
4. Michael Steinberg, liner notes to *Stravinsky in America,* 7.

piece he was setting. If the authorities were right, Stravinsky's piece is not a setting but a variation on the anthem. This issue is one for U.S. law, but in other disputed cases there may be no way of deciding a tune's identity, and therefore no way of settling a piece's status as a setting.

If a realization is to be a successful setting, it should display the tune to advantage. Sometimes this is not achieved. Stravinsky's "Star-Spangled Banner," if it is assumed to be a setting at all, does display the tune to advantage. But not all settings satisfy this condition. For example, Orlando Gibbons's setting of "The Woods So Wild" has been judged harshly by some critics. Willi Apel notes the "graceful charm and gentlemanly elegance" of the popular songs that Byrd chose as his themes, but Gibbons's variations, he says, are "beholden throughout to figuration technique, which does not lack a certain elegance, but is essentially empty."[5] In a similar vein, John Caldwell describes the setting of the song by Orlando Gibbons as "over-elaborate and inconsistent with the character of the tune"[6] (see example 3.1). Of course, an unsuccessful setting of a work may still be a successful realization of it. The distinguishing aim of settings is the way in which they *present* the material being realized. There are many ways of presenting musical material—providing it with a setting is only one of them—and different criteria for success apply in different cases.

Executive Realizations: Idealist and Realist Accounts

According to Busoni, the performance of a piece of music—which he equates with its "emotional interpretation"—aims to recover the idea that animated its composition.[7] In this respect, Busoni regards realization as having the same aim as transcription, composition, and variation. For him, the source of authority in performance is the composer's idea, not the score. Given this focus on the composer's idea, Busoni could hardly agree that the score is authoritative regarding a musical work—thinking, as he did, that

5. Apel, *History of Keyboard Music*, 279. The two sets are recorded on *William Byrd: The Complete Keyboard Music*, disc 4, track 1, and Orlando Gibbons, *Masters of Early English Keyboard Music IV: Orlando Gibbons and Giles Farnaby*, Thurston Dart, Éditions de l'oiseau-lyre OL 50131, side 1, track 4, respectively.

6. John Caldwell, *English Keyboard Music Before the Nineteenth Century* (Oxford: Blackwell, 1973), 86–87.

7. Busoni, *Sketch of a New Esthetic*, 84.

EXAMPLE 3.1 Orlando Gibbons, "The Woods So Wild"

musical notation necessarily fails to capture the composer's inspiration: "Notation, the writing out of compositions, is primarily an ingenious expedient for catching an inspiration, with the purpose of exploiting it later. But notation is to improvisation as the portrait to the living model."[8]

Accordingly, Busoni describes those for whom the score is the source of authority as "lawgivers" who demand that the performer "reproduce the rigidity of the signs." He thinks that the lawgivers' demand is inconsistent with the fluidity of artistic performance because it implies that a musical work should "always be reproduced in precisely the same tempo, whensoever, by whomsoever, and under whatever conditions it might be performed." But this demand is not realistic: "Great artists play their own works differ-

8. Ibid.

ently at each repetition, remodel them on the spur of the moment, acceler-
ate and retard, in a way which they could not indicate by signs."[9] Busoni
conflates performance and interpretation in these passages, though the
notions are distinct. We will first consider his claims in relation to performance, and only later (in Chapter 4) in relation to interpretation.

Presumably Busoni means the analogy of the portrait and the model to
remind us that a portrait can be corrected by reference to the model. Similarly, a musical score can be corrected by reference to the composer's inspiration. Of course, once the portrait has been finished, the model may skip
town—and the composer's inspiration may be just as elusive. It may not be
possible to recover the composer's inspiration, even when it *is* possible to
perform the piece. Therefore, recovery of the composer's inspiration is not
a necessary condition of performing the work with authority.

Neither is it sufficient. Busoni's idea licenses performers to disregard a
published score under certain circumstances, provided that performers claim
to have access to the composer's inspiration. But what, apart from the score,
counts as evidence of the composer's inspiration? An earlier sketch? The
composer's words? A performance by the composer? None of these is of
itself sufficient to trump the authority of the published score. The early
sketch may have been rejected or revised in the course of completing the
score. The composer's words may represent only one among a number of
possible interpretations of the work. The composer's performance at one
time may be quite different from another, as Busoni himself notes. Even if
we were able to recover evidence about the composer's inspiration, this
would not be sufficient to enable us to perform the work authoritatively. If
we wish to perform a piece of music authoritatively, then, it is neither necessary nor sufficient to aim at recovering an idea that inspired the composer. Busoni's idealist account does not survive scrutiny.

Stephen Davies would count as one of Busoni's "lawgivers." His account
of performance is realistically rooted by reference to the score. According to
him, to perform a work correctly is to (more or less) match the score's performance directives, and to do so as a result of following the score.[10] I agree
with his view that to perform a work is to comply with directives that are
enshrined in the work. Yet I wish to draw attention to a type of directive that
plays an especially important role in the performance of musical works.

9. Ibid., 84–85.
10. Davies, *Musical Works and Performances,* 152–75.

Some performance directives are merely *implicit* in the work. The distinction between explicit and implicit performance directives is decisive in distinguishing those performances that are guided by Arturo Toscanini's "objectivist" maxim, "come è scritto," from those that adopt an "authenticist" approach. The objectivist credo requires compliance with the score's explicit directives. The authenticist approach takes the work's implicit directives (such as execution on period instruments or adopting period styles, such as *notes inégales*) to be just as binding as the explicit ones. The objectivist privileges the written score over all else. The authenticist requires that the written score be supplemented by knowledge of any assumptions that the composer may have made in compiling the score but may not have bothered to make explicit. The two approaches rest on different conceptions of the musical work. To the objectivist, if something is to qualify as a musical work it must, like any work of art, have been fixed in a form that allows it to endure unchanged. In the case of the musical work, the written score provides this fixed form. The authenticist relies less on a notion of the musical work as a work of art in this sense, and instead is more concerned with the musical work as something whose "fixing" in a score provides a pragmatic precondition for its performance on particular occasions. The objectivist sees the musical work under the aspect of an entity enduring through time. The authenticist sees it under the aspect of the activities that instantiate it over time.

Some implicit performance directives direct that something *not* be done. They are implicit *proscriptions*. Sometimes a score, or a particular passage in a score, implicitly directs that in performing it we are not to add any notes. These are implicit directives to the effect that the passage in question is *saturated*, and they potentially contrast that passage with other (unsaturated) passages that allow the performer to add cadenzas, embellishments, or improvisations. Now, this distinction between saturated and unsaturated passages allows us to judge whether any extra pitches or rhythms added in performance can legitimately count as part of the realization of the passage. If the passage is saturated, any additions to the score would count as a *variation* on it, not a realization.

The distinction between saturated and unsaturated passages is not commonly thought of as applying to the instrumental music of the Romantic era. Yet the applicability of the distinction to that music is suggested by the fact that it was common for pianists at the start of the twentieth century to add extensively to the notes that can be read on the pages of Romantic piano music. For example, Theodor Leschetizky makes extensive additions

EXAMPLE 3.2 Theodor Leschetitzky, Chopin's Nocturne in D-flat Major, op. 27, no. 2

to Chopin's Nocturne in D-flat Major, op. 27, no. 2, in his 1906 Welte-Mignon piano roll (example 3.2).[11] Leschetitzky's performance goes well beyond the printed score, as Harold Schonberg notes: "Leschetitzky was the most popular, respected and productive teacher after Liszt, and he produced some of the greatest pianists of the twentieth century. And how does Leschetitzky play the nocturne? Leaving interpretive considerations aside, he introduces new harmonies, a new cadenza or two, and does quite a bit of rewriting. By present standards it is intolerable."[12]

What is the basis for Schonberg's judgment that Leschetitzky's additions are intolerable? Leschetitzky's rewriting, his ornaments, and his cadenzas are in Chopin's style, and the bass octaves convey an appropriate sense of structure. If we were talking about a vocal performance, or about an

11. Theodor Leschetitzky, perf., *Nocturne in D Flat Major, Op. 27, No. 2*, by Frédéric Chopin, on *Berühmte Pianisten um die Jahrhundertwende*, Telefunken, HT32, side 2, track 3.

12. Harold C. Schonberg, *The Great Pianists* (New York: Simon and Schuster, 1963), 132.

"authentic" rendition of a Mozart piano piece, such things would be to the performer's credit. The issue comes down to this: is this passage in Chopin's score saturated? Leschetitzky treats it as unsaturated. Schonberg takes it to be saturated, and therefore he should take Leschetitzky's performance to be a variation on the original, rather than a realization of it.

Let us return to Davies's subtle account of what is involved in performing a musical work. Davies distinguishes between the score's determinative and nondeterminative instructions, and he holds that a realization of the score is not required to follow nondeterminative instructions. Thus, for Davies, the principle that a successful realization must preserve the work's content should be understood as qualified in this way. Preservation of the work's nondeterminative content is not required for a successful realization. I wish to raise a difficulty with Davies's account, but before doing so I will discuss the relation between the determinative/nondeterminative distinction and the explicit/implicit distinction among performance directives.

The two distinctions cut across one another. Performance directives are typically explicit and determinative; some performance directives, however, are implicit and determinative. This, at any rate, is the fundamental belief of authenticists. Equally, there are nondeterminative performance directives, and these may be explicit or implicit. Some musicians regard a score's specification of instrumentation as merely advisory, and therefore as an element that can be disregarded in the realization of the work. For example, they are happy to play works written for the harpsichord on the pianoforte, provided that the music is playable on this instrument and sounds good on it. The ground for this decision is a belief that the composer's directives about the keyboard instrument to be used (whether these directives are explicit or merely implicit) are merely advisory. Bach's Goldberg variations are often played to good effect on the piano—for example, in Angela Hewitt's wonderfully musical recording, which combines a sense of dance with a meditative attitude and a suppleness of touch.[13] Yet Bach's score specifies a two-manual harpsichord. Some musicians think that the decision to play the work on the piano can be justified by appeal to the premise that a composer's specifications of the means of performance can only be advisory, and so in disregarding those specifications, we are not flouting any determinative directive concerning the execution of the work.

13. Angela Hewitt, perf., *Johann Sebastian Bach, Goldberg Variations: Aria mit verschiedenen Veränderungen ("Aria with Diverse Variations"), BWV988, Hyperion CDA 67305.

I now pass on to the difficulties with Davies's account. Davies bases the distinction between determinative and nondeterminative instructions on the supposed existence of conventions regarding musical notation:

> The composer is able to express in a musical notation many of her intentions as to the way the work is to be performed in virtue of her knowledge of notational conventions, this knowledge being held in common with musicians who perform the composer's score. According to these conventions, some of the composer's expressed intentions are determinative of what must be played in faithfully realizing the work in performance. And, according to these conventions, other of the composer's expressed intentions are commendatory only (and not determinative).[14]

Thus, whether a directive is determinative of the work depends on whether a convention exists for disregarding the directive in performing the work. For instance, Davies says: "Phrasing was not notationally determined in the early seventeenth century but was notationally determined by the nineteenth century. At some time, before the convention was established, composers notated phrasings that would have been rightly understood as recommendations for, rather than as determinative of, what should be played."[15] Elsewhere, he asserts that "by the mid-nineteenth century, notated phrasing and dynamics are determinative and must be observed in an authentic performance; in the mid-eighteenth century these musical parameters are variable within wide limits and notations of them had the status only of recommendations."[16]

Now, it is true that in seventeenth-century scores there are not very many phrasings or dynamics, but that does not mean that such markings are just recommendations. It would be a mistake to regard the dynamic markings in Bach's *Chromatic Fantasy and Fugue* as mere recommendations, just because there are few of them. On the contrary, the rarer they are, the more they command respect. Yet Davies appears to make this very slide from what is rare to what is merely advisory when he writes, for example,

---

14. Davies, "Transcription, Authenticity, and Performance," 54.

15. Davies, "Authenticity in Musical Performance," in *Themes in the Philosophy of Music*, 86.

16. Davies, "The Ontology of Musical Works and the Authenticity of Their Performances," in *Themes in the Philosophy of Music*, 76–77.

"The earlier the work, the more the score is silent, or contains advice only, about details that must be concretely realized in performance."[17]

A better basis for the notion of determinative instructions can be found in Searle and Vanderveken's account of a class of English verbs that they label directives.[18] These are distinguished from one another according to (a) whether they allow for the possibility of refusal ("tell" does not, "ask" does), (b) their strength ("command" is stronger than "urge"), and (c) the goodness in general, or the goodness for the hearer, of the action directed ("recommend," unlike "advise," presupposes that the action is good in general). If we agree that musical scores function as directives in this general sense, that leaves open the question of whether they allow for the possibility of refusal, how strong they are, and whether the performative actions that they specify are supposed to be good in general or simply good for the performers. Searle and Vanderveken distinguish two independent sources of a directive's degree of strength: "the intensity of the speaker's desire that the hearer should do the directed act, and the extent of the speaker's authority or power over the hearer."[19] I believe that the question of the strength of the score's directives is a question of authority, not of desire, and Davies, too, acknowledges this: "Whether an intention issues in an instruction that must be obeyed, as against a recommendation that might be ignored by the performer, is not a matter of the strength with which the composer wills that intention."[20]

Rather, it is a matter of the composer's authority,[21] and authority consists of "a right ... to decide on matters within a given area."[22] A score's determinative directives, then, are those on which the composer has a right to decide. Whether a particular score contains any directives that are not determinative in this sense depends on whether it contains any directives about matters on which the composer had no right to decide. Such cases might occur when composers pen scores for instruments about whose playing technique they have inadequate knowledge. (Imagine, for example,

17. Davies, *Musical Works and Performances*, 212. Nor, of course, does it mean that the numerous dynamic markings and phrasings in twentieth-century scores are all determinative of the scored works: one has only to think of the numerous markings in Longo's edition of Scarlatti's sonatas, which cannot have any status other than as recommendations.

18. Searle and Vanderveken, *Foundations of Illocutionary Logic*, 198–205.

19. Ibid., 100.

20. Davies, *Musical Works and Performances*, 211.

21. Ibid., 213.

22. Mautner, *Penguin Dictionary of Philosophy*, 53.

that Brahms had not consulted Joachim when composing his Violin Concerto. We do not know what the work would have been like, but we can guess that violinists would have regarded it as lacking in the authority that it now possesses.) In my opinion, Davies's account is best modified so as to base the idea of a determinative directive on that of authority rather than on a notion of convention. The modified account provides an adequate conceptual framework for thinking about musical performances.

To my mind, Angela Hewitt's performance of the Goldberg Variations on the piano is not an authentic performance. If the notion of a determinative directive is based (as I think it should be) on that of the composer's authority, then it can hardly be denied that Bach's directive to play the work on a two-manual harpsichord is determinative. And if (as I believe) an authentic realization is one that complies with the work's determinative directives, then a performance of the Goldbergs on the piano is not an authentic performance *tout court*. At the same time, it may be authentic in certain respects. For example, it may include all and only the right notes, and it may respect the score's tempo markings. As for Leschetitzky's Chopin, it may, for all I know, be perfectly authentic. It would be so if the passages that Leschetitzky decorates could be shown to be unsaturated. In either case, of course, what is not an authentic realization may be aesthetically effective.

Musicians hold different opinions about whether repeats marked in a musical score constitute determinative directives. Alfred Cortot, for instance, in his *Édition de travail* of Chopin's *Funeral March* Sonata, states that the exposition repeat in the first movement is obligatory.[23] Taking a different tack, Davies offers the following reasoning on the issue of exposition repeats: "If they served originally to help first-time audiences, many of whom would not be paying close attention anyway, to grasp the main thematic ideas, and if ignoring them does not unbalance the movement or its relation to other movements, their observance is unnecessary now because the audience is likely to be conversant with the work or to listen intently."[24] He does not say what would follow if exposition repeats did *not* originally have this function. To this extent, his account is incomplete. Nevertheless, it is clear that he thinks that marked exposition repeats are not always determinative.

23. Alfred Cortot, arr., *Édition de travail des oeuvres de Chopin: Sonate Op. 35* (Paris: Éditions Salabert, 1930), 1. Cortot doesn't play the repeat in his 1933 recording: Alfred Cortot, perf., *Chopin, Piano Concerto No. 2, Sonatas 2 and 3*, Allegro CDO 3037.
24. Davies, *Musical Works and Performances*, 213–14.

According to Jerrold Levinson, exposition repeats have a purely musical function, independent of whether the context is that of a first or a later performance: "Since the development in such pieces generally commences in the dominant or some other nontonic key, the particular quality of the progression from the end of exposition to beginning of development (e.g., V → V) is weakened if the listener is not given, earlier on, the contrasting progression from end of exposition to beginning of exposition (V → I), when the repeat is taken."[25] This gives a good musical reason why composers in the classical period should have directed that exposition repeats be taken. In the light of Levinson's view, I do not see how it can be disputed that the composer has the right to say whether there should be an exposition repeat. (Of course it is another question whether, in a particular score, the repeat sign is used for this purpose.) To my mind, it follows that a score's repeats are determinative of the notated work. It also follows that a work that does not observe determinative repeats cannot be an authentic one, even if it has many authentic aspects and even if, aesthetically, it is satisfying. For instance, Cortot does not play Chopin's first-movement exposition repeat in his 1933 recording, and his performance ought therefore to be regarded as lacking authenticity by anyone who (like Cortot himself) takes the exposition repeat to be determinative.

Similar conclusions apply to other cuts in performance. Chopin's Scherzo in B Minor, op. 20, is a work that seems hardly ever to have been performed without cuts in the early part of the twentieth century. For example, bars 129 to 244 are cut by Fannie Bloomfield Zeisler in her 1912 Welte-Mignon piano roll,[26] and by Josef Hofmann in his 1923 disc[27] and his 1926 Duo-art piano roll.[28] Alfred Cortot, in his 1933 edition of the Scherzos, describes this cut as sanctioned by "une tradition d'usage presque constant," and the evidence seems to support his claim.[29] But it is another question whether the cut is justified, and yet another question whether it is justified because the composer's inclusion of those bars in the score was nondeterminative.

25. Jerrold Levinson, *Music in the Moment* (Ithaca: Cornell University Press, 1997), 84 n. 6.

26. Fannie Bloomfield Zeisler, perf., *Fannie Bloomfield Zeisler, 1863–1927*, Pierian 0003/4, disc 1, track 3.

27. Josef Hofmann, perf., *Great Pianists of the 20th Century: Josef Hofmann*, Philips 456 835–2, disc 2, track 17.

28. Josef Hofmann, perf., *Grand Piano: Josef Hofmann*, Nimbus NI 8803, track 11.

29. Alfred Cortot, arr., *Édition de travail des oeuvres de Chopin: Scherzos* (Paris: Éditions Salabert, 1933), 6 n. 13.

Cortot attempts to justify the cut on aesthetic grounds, saying that it is a mere repetition of what has been heard already, which he thinks inappropriate in this "exalted" music, making a comparison with speeches by Phaedra or Othello: "On s'imagine mal Phèdre exhalant par deux fois, et dans les memes termes, sa plainte désespérée ou Othello, son orageuse passion."

But this argument proves too much: it would justify the omission of all *da capo* repeats in opera. In any case, it has no bearing on the question of authority, and therefore does not show that the cutting of whole passages from a work can be justified on the ground that those passages were merely optional—assuming that the score does not include any indication to that effect. At the same time, the work may still be able to be realized in an aesthetically satisfying way by a performance that makes these cuts.

Representation

Whether they are settings or quotations or sketches for a performance, or whether they are executive realizations, musical realizations are always intentional representations of the works they realize. In all cases, the realization contains the work, and because of that, there is necessarily a mapping from some of its elements onto the work's elements. These elements include some of the realization's notes. And in that mapping, the notes in the realization are generally *the same* as the notes in the work. So the function that maps elements of the realization onto elements of the work is an identity-function. If it were otherwise—if the notes played were to correspond to the notes in the work in other ways (for instance, as inversions or retrogrades)—then the musician's actions would not be a realization of the work, though they would still constitute an executive representation of the work.

In a realization, there is always an agent of representation who sets up the vehicle to represent the object—whether this be the arranger of the setting, the composer who inserts a quotation into a larger work, the editor of a marked-up score, or the performer. In this last case, the audience is invited, in a context of generally understood performance conventions, to take the realization as an instance of the work. Many explicit signs indicate the intended status of the musicians' actions as a realization of the work. Posters, program notes, or the performers' live comments declare that what is to occur will be a representation of a given work. Moreover, audiences are accustomed to abstracting from the performance's unintentional departures from the work so that the intended representational object may be identified with the work.[30]

Realizations are like transcriptions and unlike variations in that they highlight resemblances with their object rather than differences from it. Realizations differ from both transcriptions and variations, though, in that they augment their object rather than substituting for parts of it. Realizations, variations, and transcriptions all have musical content for their object of representation; realizations differ from variations and transcriptions in that their vehicle is an action sequence, not another musical content.

Musical realizations are commonly experiential representations, making their representational objects recognizable in the realization. This is essential to some types of realization, though not to all. Notational realizations generally aim to provide experiential representations of their parent works—whether the experience in question is one of reading the score or of listening to the music. Someone who reads music, and who is familiar with the original work, will generally have no difficulty recognizing it in a notational realization; someone who is familiar with the sounds of the original will generally have no difficulty hearing them in performances that execute a notational realization. Nonetheless, a successful setting or quotation might well hide its tune within the realization, or make it unrecognizable in other ways. In such a case, we could still say that there is a realization of the work, though not an experiential one, just as we were prepared to talk of non-experiential variations. There is, however, one class of realizations for which experiential representation is essential—namely, those executive realizations whose aim is not merely to play the musical work but to project it to an audience. Such realizations are commonly called performances, and they should be distinguished from mere playings. The reason why performances must be experiential realizations of the work performed is precisely that they aim to project the work, and projection implies recognition. A work that is realized in such a way that it cannot be recognized may have been played, but cannot have been performed.

Treatment

Because the content of a score is relatively abstract, its realization inevitably makes its content more concrete, and thus the process of realization neces-

---

30. Paul Thom, "On Changing the Subject," *Metaphilosophy* 31 (2001): 64.

sarily involves going beyond what is specified in the score. In certain cases, one can discern in the realization of the score a *treatment* of the work.

When a score is annotated preparatory to performance, the treatment of its material may be purely local, as when Cortot in his 1930s series of *Éditions de travail* realizes bar 609 of Chopin's B Minor Scherzo in a way that substitutes broken octaves for Chopin's double chromatic scale.[31] This realization does not seem to be connected with anything else in the work and appears to be motivated solely by a desire for a flashy finish. The case is different with Cortot's realization of Chopin's *Funeral March* Sonata. Cortot writes an illuminating preface to the Sonata, subjoining to the musical text an interpretive commentary designed to assist the performer in coming to an interpretation of the work and effectively practicing the music. What Cortot brings to the edition is, first of all, his authoritative musicianship and deep practical knowledge of the music, but he also draws on his considerable literary and critical skills. In the preface, Cortot takes up Anton Rubinstein's description of the Sonata as a "poem of death," adding that the interpretation of the work requires one to use one's imagination: "For our part we accept the poetic given imagined by Rubinstein. For (to take up a phrase of Saint-Saëns) we see what the interpretation can gain from it, and we don't see what it can lose."[32]

Traditionally, this interpretation understands the Sonata's Finale as representing the wind howling over tombstones. Cortot endorses this view, writing of "the bitter shuddering of the hallucinatory finale, the whirling of the wind of death, the wind over graves." Chopin himself is said to have dismissed this interpretation, saying that the movement was nothing more than two hands babbling in unison;[33] Liszt also rejected it as an unwarranted literary intrusion.[34] Cortot himself admits that the interpretation may not "authentically translate the composer's idea," but he thinks that "it is nonetheless perfectly applicable." In line with this global interpretation, Cortot recommends that the Finale be played *una corda* and without sustaining pedal, but with a sudden *crescendo* to *fortissimo* in bar 13 from the end.[35]

Cortot, in his 1933 recording, follows his own prescriptions about this passage, although there is no logical necessity that he should have done so (as is evident from the fact that while he says the repeat in the first movement

31. Cortot, *Édition de travail: Scherzos*, 22.
32. Cortot, *Édition de travail: Sonate Op. 35*, i.
33. Ibid., 30.
34. Rosen, *The Romantic Generation*, 298.
35. Cortot, *Édition de travail: Sonate Op. 35*, 30–35.

of this Sonata is obligatory,[36] he does not play it in his recording). The effect is startling. To someone familiar with the wind-over-gravestones interpretation, Cortot's sudden *crescendo* lends a Gothic tone to the prevailing atmosphere of "sinister, repressed excitement."[37] Cortot himself plays on this Gothic tone in his use of the lurid phrase "a movement of inflexible gyration."[38] Cortot's realization of Chopin's Finale can be regarded as an aspectual representation, to be heard as the winds over the tombstones, given the context in which Cortot espouses an overall interpretation of the Sonata as a poem of death.

Consider, now, musical settings. A setting may embody a treatment, by virtue of the fact that it confirms a piece's defining qualities, as does Berlioz's setting of "La Marseillaise." Alternatively, a setting may endow the piece with unexpected qualities, as does Bach's setting of the final Chorale in his Cantata no. 149, "Man singet mit Freuden vom Sieg," where the simple orchestration of the chorale tune is augmented at the very last bar by three trumpets and tympani, bringing the Cantata to a triumphant close (example 3.3). In both cases, the setting involves a metaphorical transfiguration of the music. Berlioz transforms the popular song into a high-art expression of the spirit of political revolution. Bach transforms the congregation's humble chorale into a momentary vision of eternal life.

Similarly, a musical quotation may embody an aspectual treatment of the material quoted. It may cover that material in a blaze of glory, as Brahms does in his orchestration of the student drinking-song "Gaudeamus igitur" at the close of his *Academic Festival Overture*. Or the treatment may be satirical, as when Berlioz quotes the "Dies irae" (set for the "coarse, vulgar sound" of the ophicleide[39]) in his *Fantastic Symphony*.

An executive realization may incorporate a treatment of the music being played, either at the local level or globally. Carl Flesch described a performance by Fritz Kreisler in these startling terms: "It was an unrestrained orgy of sinfully seductive sounds, depravedly fascinating," and "a sensuality intensified to the point of frenzy."[40] These descriptions suggest that the vio-

36. Ibid., 1.

37. Rosen, *The Romantic Generation*, 300.

38. Cortot, *Édition de travail: Sonate Op. 35*, 35.

39. Hugh Macdonald, liner notes to *Symphonie Fantastique*, by Hector Berlioz, The London Classical Players, Roger Norrington, EMI CDC 7 49541 2, 5.

40. Quoted in Harvey Sachs, *Virtuoso: The Life and Art of Niccolò Paganini, Franz Liszt, Anton Rubinstein, Ignace Jan Paderewski, Fritz Kreisler, Pablo Casals, Wanda Landowska, Vladimir Horowitz, Glenn Gould* (London: Thames and Hudson, 1982), 123, 128.

EXAMPLE 3.3　Johann Sebastian Bach, Chorale from Cantata no. 149, "Man singet mit Freuden vom Sieg"

linist was applying a global treatment of a particularly sensual nature to the music performed.

Among the global treatments that individual performers apply generally to the works in their repertoire, a special place is occupied by certain personal "trademark" qualities that mark all or most of their performances—qualities such as Toscanini's electricity or Vladimir Horowitz's bravado. Roland Barthes has written about the unique aesthetic qualities of singers under the title "The Grain of the Voice."[41] He focuses attention on the

41. Roland Barthes, "The Grain of the Voice," in *Image-Music-Text: Essays Selected and Translated by Stephen Heath* (London: Fontana, 1977), 183–85.

French singer Charles Panzéra. A more familiar example to contemporary English-speaking lovers of singing might be provided by Billie Holiday. Gunther Schuller writes about the unique timbre of her voice:

> This was an innate gift, God-given, if you will, certainly one of her natural physical attributes.... The reedy timbre—akin to that of an English horn—became its dominant quality.... In some songs (like *I Can't Believe You're in Love with Me*) her voice could be soft-spoken and subdued, like a quietly muted trumpet; in others her voice could get gritty and tart (as in *These Foolish Things* and *What a Little Moonlight Can Do*). At still other times she could take the grit right out of her voice (as in the 1937 *They Can't Take That Away from Me*), singing with a warm gentle timbre, as pure as the driven snow.[42]

An innate gift there certainly was, but, as Schuller himself shows in this commentary, the singer did many different things with that gift.

Incoherence, Illumination, Transformation, Parody

Some performances fail to achieve any global treatment of the music performed. This was the way Schonberg thought of Horowitz's various performances of the Chopin G Minor Ballade: "Horowitz fought this ballade all his life, constantly playing and recording it, never really making up his mind about how it should go."[43] He quotes with approval a reviewer who described Horowitz's performance as "a collection of details" and "inexplicable."[44] The use of these terms of disapprobation implies that Schonberg thought of Horowitz's performances of this piece as lacking in coherence.

By contrast, successful artistic realizations apply a global treatment to a work. The treatment may be related to the work in different ways, depending on what it acknowledges as the work's content and what its attitude is to that content. First, the realization may illuminate the work, by acknowledging some of its features and highlighting them in new and favorable ways. Second, the realization may transform the work by ignoring some of

42. Schuller, *The Swing Era*, 537.
43. Harold C. Schonberg, *Horowitz: His Life and Music* (London: Simon and Schuster, 1992), 326.
44. Ibid., 251.

its features and turning it into something that it was not. Let us consider these possibilities in turn.

Earlier we noted the differences between objectivists and authenticists. Notwithstanding their differences, both groups share a motivation to illuminate works from the past. To the authenticists, those works' manner of performance has been lost sight of over time. An authentic performance does not simply uncover those implicit understandings and comply with them, but also does so in a historical setting where that compliance has recently been lacking.[45] To the objectivists, a respectful following of the published score is required, not a search for what might be implicit but unwritten in the score.

Yet another type of illuminating realization depends for its force on certain ephemeral features of the very act of performance, such as the performers' bodily gestures and facial expressions. Projection of a musical realization can be enhanced by such gestures and expressions. Indeed, the art of the conductor is in part an art of such performative enhancement— but it is not only conductors who make use of this art. This is evident in the video of pianist Lang Lang's Carnegie Hall premier recital, especially in the pianist's thrilling rendition of Liszt's *Don Giovanni* paraphrase.[46] In the "La ci darèm la mano" section, Lang mimes the parts of the Don and Zerlina most convincingly. There is not so much a question of a mimetic accompaniment to a musical performance, or a musical accompaniment to a pantomime, as an integrated performance having both musical and mimetic aspects. Lang's whole performance illuminates the Liszt-Mozart work in a strikingly original way, because while the piano playing sounds entirely Western, the performance's visual, mimetic aspect displays the performer's Chinese heritage in a most captivating way. The expressions and gestures seem to hail from the world of Chinese opera, and yet they seem to integrate perfectly with the music being performed.

A musician's treatment of musical material may utterly transform that material. A well-known example is Elvis Presley's 1956 version of the Leiber-Stoller song "Hound Dog."[47] Presley transforms what had been a rhythm-and-blues number into the rock-and-roll song that has since become *the* version of "Hound Dog." He made changes to the lyrics, and to the pitches

45. Thom, *For an Audience*, 81.

46. Lang Lang, perf., *Lang Lang Live at Carnegie Hall: Schumann, Haydn, Schubert, Tan Dun, Chopin, Liszt,* Deutsche Grammophon DJ-503.

47. Elvis Presley, perf., *Presley: The All-Time Greatest Hits,* RCA ND 9000, disc 1, track 3.

and rhythms, as executed by Big Mama Thornton on her 1952 recording.[48] But it is not these changes that I have in mind when I speak of a transformation; it is the song's aesthetic qualities. Mike Stoller wanted, and got, Big Mama to "growl" the song.[49] By contrast, Elvis "snarled and smirked and grunted."[50] And while the original version expressed "a grievance," the new version was "a tirade of unfocussed aggression, of all-purpose, sneering rebellion."[51] Presley's physical performance of the song, in which his "body jolted, his shoulders jerked, the hips and groin gyrated,"[52] was perfectly integrated with his vocal rendition. It was not merely his singing that transformed the original song, but the total performance.

The third type of transformation is illustrated by Glenn Gould's 1967 recording of Beethoven's *Appassionata* Sonata.[53] He plays the first movement at an extraordinarily slow pace, taking fifteen minutes to get through what most pianists do in eight or nine minutes. Some critics saw this approach as one of deliberate sabotage,[54] a description that Gould himself seemed to endorse in his sleeve notes to the record:

> The so-called *Appassionata* Sonata, Op. 57, is usually ranked with the most popular of Beethoven's keyboard works. But I confess the reasons for its popularity elude me. The *Appassionata,* in common with most of the works that Beethoven wrote in the first decade of the nineteenth century, is a study in thematic tenacity. . . . For at this period of his life Beethoven was not only preoccupied with motivic frugality; he was also preoccupied with being Beethoven. And there is about the *Appassionata* an egoistic pomposity, a defiant "let's just see if I can't get away with using that *once more*" attitude, that on my own private Beethoven poll places this sonata somewhere between the *King Stephen* Overture and the *Wellington's Victory* Symphony.[55]

48. Willie Mae Thornton, perf., *Big Mama Thornton: The Original Hound Dog,* Peacock Ace CDCHD 940, track 1.

49. Nicholas Barber, "Hound Dog," in *Lives of the Great Songs: The Greatest Pop Song Stories Collection—Ever!* ed. Tim De Lisle (London: Penguin Books, 1994), 203.

50. Ibid., 206.

51. Ibid., 204, 206.

52. Samuel Roy, *Elvis: Prophet of Power* (Brookline, Mass.: Branden, 1985), 18.

53. Glenn Gould, perf., *Beethoven Piano Sonatas, Vol. 2,* Sony SM3K 52642, disc 1, tracks 5–7.

54. Michael Stegemann, liner notes to *Beethoven Piano Sonatas,* 7.

55. Quoted in ibid., 7–8.

If one had listened to Gould's performance without being aware of these critical comments, it might have sounded like someone practicing, or else like someone making fun of the music. But the pianist's critical comments make it clear that he has a serious view about the music, even if that view is an iconoclastic one, and his realization of the music can be heard as one informed by that view and as an attempt to persuade the listener of the view's cogency. Gould's performance is an effective realization of the movement thus conceived.

Summary

The process of realization, whether in the form of a setting or a quotation or the marking-up of a score or an actual performance, differs from transcription and variation in that it makes the abstract concrete, whereas the latter activities substitute one set of elements for another in a concrete original. The product itself also differs: executive realizations are action sequences, unlike transcriptions and variations, which are musical works. Nonetheless, the structure of intentional representation is present in all these cases.

Busoni's idealist account of the executive realization of a work—as being aimed at recovering the composer's inspiration—is neither necessary nor sufficient for the authoritative realization of a musical work. A realist account, in terms of executing a musical score's determinative directives, is both necessary and sufficient for correct realization, provided that it treats determinativeness as a matter of authority rather than convention.

The representation of a work in an executive realization is commonly experiential. Yet there is no absolute requirement that it be so, except in the case of performances (as opposed to mere playings) of a work. A realization may make cuts or adapt the work for instruments other than those specified in the score. Cuts (including cutting repeats or dynamics), or adaptations of the work to means of performance not specified by the work, generally conflict with a work's determinative directives, but taken individually they do not compromise the work's recognizability. While they compromise authenticity in performance, they do not necessarily compromise the realization's aesthetic success.

Among a work's directives, some are merely implicit. We can distinguish the authenticists' approach to realizations from that of the objectivists by reference to such implicit directives. Some of these directives direct the nonexecution of certain things, which is crucial in deciding the extent to which the work (or an individual passage in it) is saturated. Such decisions have consequences for whether we treat certain performances as realizations of or variations on the original work. A performative realization may or may not include an aspectual treatment of the realized work. The performative treatment of a musical work may illuminate the work, or it may transform or undermine it.

Interpretations

What has all this to do with interpretation? The musical activities thus far described seem quite different from the activities that philosophers classify as interpretative. Many philosophers subscribe to a narrow concept of interpretation, according to which critical interpretations are paradigmatic. Interpreters, on this view, are in the primary sense writers or speakers. Jerrold Levinson advances this view in his article "Performative vs. Critical Interpretation in Music." According to Levinson, critical interpretation is "what we tend to understand by 'interpretation' when no qualification is given." A critical interpretation is a statement providing "an account of a work's import and functioning."[1]

One consequence of this view is that musical works (including transcriptions and variations) cannot without qualification count as instances of interpretation, and neither can performances, because in neither case do we have something that is *eo ipso* a critical interpretation. Critics (and, in a derivative way, listeners) may interpret musical works; composers, including those who compose transcriptions and variations, do not, as such, interpret

---

1. Jerrold Levinson, "Performative vs. Critical Interpretation in Music," in *The Interpretation of Music*, ed. Michael Krausz (Oxford: Clarendon Press, 1993), 33, 34.

anything. They only do so when they speak or write about the music they compose. Similarly, an act could not of itself, strictly speaking, be an interpretation, though it might embody one or be thought to embody one. If, as Levinson says, a performative interpretation is merely "a considered way of playing a piece of music,"[2] then clearly a performative interpretation is not *eo ipso* a critical interpretation. Moreover, there is (according to Levinson) no way of assigning "a definite correlative" critical interpretation to a given performative interpretation.[3] In fact, Levinson finds no systematic relation between the two types of interpretation. On the contrary, it appears that for him, there are fundamental differences between them. In the light of such fundamental differences, it seems to me that Levinson, in the end, is left saying that it is merely "a curious fact" that performative interpretation is called interpretation at all.[4]

Another consequence, as Levinson elaborates his view, is that interpretation—namely, critical interpretation—aims to be true and definitive. In Levinson's view, "performative interpretations irreducibly compete for space in a way that individually valid but superficially opposed critical interpretations, when properly understood as partial, do not."[5] Conflicting critical interpretations of the same object, according to him, should be synthesized into one overall critical interpretation accounting for the work's import and functioning while acknowledging its ambiguities, whereas performative interpretations of the same work are inherently plural.

These differences are admitted, but my argument will be that there are also deep similarities between certain musical phenomena and the activities of interpreters—and that there is a concept of interpretation, more liberal than Levinson's, that embraces certain activities of composers and performers alongside critical interpretations. Indeed, in some ways, the musical activities will turn out to be paradigmatic instances of interpretation.

A Concept of Interpretation

Any interpretation has an object—that of which it is an interpretation. The interpretation is made by an interpreter. What is made must in some ways exceed the object; because of this, interpretation involves creativity. The interpretation cannot simply reproduce the object, but it does repre-

2. Ibid., 36.
3. Ibid., 44.
4. Ibid., 33.
5. Ibid., 39.

sent the object, and because of this fact, interpretation requires fidelity to the object. (Notice that we have not specified the ontological category of that which represents or of that which is represented.) This representation is an interpretation of the object, provided it says that the object has a certain meaning, or shows the object as having a certain meaning. (I am using "meaning" in a broad sense, so that the meaning of a piece of music is whatever we understand when we understand the music.)

It might be objected that such a concept of interpretation is no concept at all, because to say that an interpretation *either* states that the object has a certain meaning *or* shows the object as having that meaning is to present a formulation that is irreducibly disjunctive. There is, it might be said, nothing genuinely in common between these disjuncts. This indeed was the point of drawing a sharp distinction between critical and performative interpretations.

In reply, it might be said that a genuine concept need not be such that its instances all have something in common, provided that the instances are connected by relations of derivation (as, for example, is the case for the concept of family resemblance). And even if there is nothing in common between saying and showing, still, we can construe one as derivative of the other. For example, it might be said that showing is as if stating, and thus the concept of showing is derivative of that of stating.

Or we might say that there is indeed something in common between saying and showing: in both cases, a propositional content is presented for consideration. This is genuinely something in common, even given that there is also a genuine difference between asserting a propositional content as true and considering a propositional content as an imaginative construct. In the end, however, it must be admitted that these considerations are not final. The proposed concept could be resisted by someone intent on preserving an unbridgeable dichotomy between critical and performative interpretations.

If the broad concept of interpretation *is* admitted, however, it follows that interpretation occurs in a wide range of cases. Here are some examples.

(a) When a philologist restores a corrupt or damaged text by correcting and completing it, the reconstituted whole is construed as showing the text's meaning.

(b) When a psychologist explains puzzling behavior by hypothesizing its underlying psychological states, a new totality is constructed, which by contextualizing the behavior shows its meaning.

(c) When a preacher applies the utterances of Holy Writ to contemporary everyday situations, he or she integrates the original text into a whole that incorporates those situations, and this totality is taken to show the text as having a meaning that was not previously explicit.

(d) When an inspired theater director arrives at a new "take" on a work for performance, by giving it a new setting or by costuming it in a new way, the original work becomes part of a newly constructed whole that shows it as having a new meaning.

(e) Critical interpretations are like this, too, if they state or show what meaning or meanings the object of interpretation has.

All these cases fit our concept of interpretation, and in each case the interpreter proceeds by way of a representation of the object. The philologist restoring a corrupt or damaged text characteristically takes certain elements from the text (those that are not corrupt) and incorporates them in a reconstructed text. Other elements in the text (those that are corrupt) will be modified in the reconstruction. Yet other elements will be added in the reconstruction, where the text is incomplete. There are, then, mappings from elements of the reconstruction onto elements of the text. In some cases the mappings are based on identities, and in others, on correspondences of nonidentical elements. The philologist postulates a relationship between the reconstruction as a whole and the text, on the basis of which the reconstruction shows the text as having a particular meaning. Such a postulation might be warranted by empirical evidence to the effect that the modifications made by the interpreter reverse the actual processes by which the text was corrupted or damaged. Because the reconstruction maps onto the text, and because of its postulated global relationship with the text, the reconstruction functions as a representation of the text.

In a somewhat similar manner, the psychologist explaining puzzling behavior combines certain of its elements (those that can be taken at face value) with modifications of other elements (those that are taken to mask covert psychological processes). Further elements are added, with a view to reconstructing an intelligible totality of which the overt behavior is a part. This totality is related to the unexplained behavior as a representation of it: there are mappings from some of its elements onto (identical or modified) elements of the unexplained behavior, and the reconstructed whole is judged by the psychologist to show the behavior's meaning. This judgment might be warranted by empirical evidence to the effect that the modifications that the psychologist introduces reflect the ways in which psychological processes are actually masked or suppressed.

The preacher applying a sacred text to everyday situations engages in a similar process. Some of the text's elements are read literally, others allegorically; all are integrated into an intelligible present-day context. Again, this totality is related to the original text as a representation of it: there are mappings from some of its elements onto (identical or modified) elements of the text, and the reconstructed whole is judged by the preacher to show the text as having a contemporary meaning. Whether the preacher's judgment is a reasonable one depends on whether it is plausible to postulate a deep meaning that is shared by the original text and the contemporary application.

The theater director preparing a work for performance under a rereading takes certain elements in the work (those that are to be performed as the work dictates) and incorporates them, unchanged, into a production script. Other elements in the work are modified in the reconstruction. Yet other elements will be added in the reconstruction. There are, then, mappings from elements of the reconstruction onto elements of the work. In some cases, the mappings are based on identity; in others, on the director's alterations to the work. Jonathan Miller explains the process, referring to his Mafioso reinterpretation of Giuseppe Verdi's *Rigoletto:* "I have worked by a principle comparable to the mathematical one of mapping. You take two sets and see whether in fact they map without undue force being applied. Here the social world of the original court mapped completely, without any of the points having to be dislocated, on to the social world of the Mafia."[6] The director postulates a global relationship—a deep sharing of meanings— between the production script and the original work. Miller elaborates: "I noticed how consistent the plot was with something that could have taken place in another Italian community where people have absolute power of life and death over others, namely the world of the Godfather and the Italian Mafia."[7] Because the reinterpretation maps onto the work, and because of its postulated global relationship with the work, the reinterpretation functions as a representation of the work.

The critic articulating the meaning or meanings of a work of art may operate by way of setting up correspondences between elements of the work

6. Jonathan Miller, *Subsequent Performances* (London: Faber and Faber, 1986), 183.
7. Ibid.

and elements of an interpretation, in the manner described disparagingly by Susan Sontag: "Directed to art, interpretation means plucking a set of elements (the X, the Y, the Z, and so forth) from the whole work. The task of interpretation is virtually one of translation. The interpreter says, Look, don't you see that X is really—or, really means—A? That Y is really B? That Z is really C?"[8] But even if the critic does not operate in this way, representation and interpretation are still in play. The critic, just as much as any other interpreter, integrates the object of interpretation into a meaning-giving context, even if all of the work's elements enter into that context unchanged. So, even if the critic does not operate in the manner Sontag describes, there is still a mapping from elements of the interpretation onto elements of the work, and there is still a global relationship between the interpretation and the work, such that the interpretation is seen as stating or showing the work's meaning or meanings. Because of all this, critical interpretations should also be seen as resting on representations of their objects. All these representations are aspectual, in so far as they apply a coherent treatment to the object of interpretation.

Interpretation is constrained partly by a concern for fidelity and partly by a need for creativity. The poles of fidelity and creativity are a little like the two excessive states, in Aristotle's ethical theory, between which virtue is found as a mean. Overdone fidelity, in the form of mere repetition or literal transcription, is not interpretation. Mere willful departures from the object are not interpretation either. Genuine interpretation lies somewhere between these extremes.

Nonetheless, reinterpretation does, in certain cases, amount to interpretation. For example, Elvis Presley's reinterpretation of the song "Hound Dog," even though it abandons many features of the original, can be heard as releasing an energy that was latent in the original. To hear it that way is to hear it as showing the song's meaning as bound up with that energy.[9]

Keeping this broad concept of interpretation in mind, I believe we can avoid the conclusion that it is merely a curious fact that performative interpretation goes by the same name that applies to critical interpretation. On the contrary, we can show that some compositions, and some performances, fall naturally under the broad concept of interpretation I have outlined.

---

8. Susan Sontag, *Against Interpretation and Other Essays* (New York: Delta, 1961), 5.
9. Thom, *Making Sense*, 98–101.

Transcriptions

On this model of interpretation, we can show that some of the transcriptions we considered in Chapter 1 count as interpretations. In order to show this, it would suffice to show that the transcriber makes a representation of the transcribed work, which displays the work as possessing a certain musical meaning, under constraints of fidelity and creativity. This is precisely what some of those transcriptions do.

We have seen already that the activity of transcription exhibits much of the structure of interpretation. The interpreter is the transcriber. The object of interpretation is the music to be transcribed, and this is normally a scored musical work, not (as Busoni would have us believe) a postulated idea in the composer's mind. The transcription is an experiential representation of that object.

It might seem overly generous to apply the term "representation" to a piece like Walsh's transcription of the *Esther* Overture (example 1.4), which appears to represent its model by simply reproducing it. This appearance is misleading, however. We must remember that the score of the original Overture specifies not just pitches and rhythms but also instrumentation; the latter specifications are omitted in Walsh's transcriptions, being replaced by the specification of a keyboard instrument. So Walsh's transcription — even though it is a literal one — actually represents the original music not by reproducing it but by means of processes of deletion and supplementation. The same applies to other transcriptions — such as Liszt's Beethoven partitions (example 1.7) or Webern's Bach Ricercar (example 1.9) — that exactly reproduce the original work's pitches and rhythms. Except for one type of case, a transcription cannot represent its original by reproducing all the original specifications, because some of those specifications identify the medium in which the music is to be performed, and the transcription is for a different medium. (The exception occurs when the new medium *includes* the original one, as, for example, if a work for solo violin were transcribed for violin and viola. Yet even in this type of case, the transcription does not represent its model by reproducing it.)

In a minimal sense, every transcription, by being an experiential representation of its parent work, functions as an interpretation of that work because it shows the work as having a musical meaning, even if that meaning is simply the necessary product of expressing the work's original meanings in a new medium. Walsh's transcriptions of Handel are of this sort. But beyond

such minimal cases, some transcriptions function as aspectual representations of the work. These cases have a stronger claim to the title of interpretations, because they generate musical meanings in a more robust sense.

Many transcriptions aim to apply a treatment (an aspectual representation) to their objects, and while some of these succeed, some do not. As we
saw in Chapter 1, some of Godowsky's Bach transcriptions cannot be said
to succeed in applying a treatment to their material, if we demand that a
genuine treatment be coherent (see example 1.11). We distinguished two
broad types of treatment, depending on whether the original material is
illuminated or transformed. Both of these types of treatment involve the
generation of musical meaning—and therefore of an interpretation. Glenn
Gould's transcription of Wagner's *Die Meistersinger* Prelude for many-handed
piano illuminates the work's contrapuntal structures. To illuminate a work
in this way is certainly to show part of its musical meaning. The same
applies to transformative transcriptions. These transformations transform
the musical meanings of the parent work. It is clear, then, that they show
the work as having certain meanings. In either case, because the transcription represents the work and shows it as having certain meanings, it counts
as an interpretation of the work. Transformative transcriptions may present
the work in a positive light, by highlighting some of its original aesthetic
qualities and expressing them in a new medium, as Busoni does with the
Bach Chaconne (example 1.2). Roger Scruton writes eloquently about these
qualities. Of Bach's original version he writes:

> This is undoubtedly one of the most noble and profound utter-
> ances for solo violin in the history of music, and a remarkable study
> in implied harmony. Its effect of titanic strain, as of a giant Atlas,
> bearing the burden of the world's great sadness, is inseparable from
> the way in which the performer must stretch across the four strings
> of the instrument, to provide as many voices as can be produced
> by it, and to imply as many more. The performer's effort must be
> heard in the music, but heard too as *part* of the music.[10]

Scruton finds these same qualities in Brahms's transcription for left hand.
Of the Busoni transcription he writes: "Busoni attempts something similar;
although, in order to make the music sound as though it is reaching beyond
the instrument, to a vaster space which cannot be captured by it, he must

10. Scruton, *The Aesthetics of Music*, 452.

add embellishments of his own, massive octave doublings, chords of a vast-ness that all but drown the melodic line."[11] The transformation may also present the music in a negative light, as Tatum does in *Elegy* (example 1.13).

The meanings that are conveyed by a transformative transcription may be richly layered, as in Liszt's transcriptions of the Beethoven symphonies, which are *inter alia* a homage to the supreme musical artist:[12] "the name of Beethoven," says Liszt in his preface, "is sacred in art." In addition to that, we find the values of virtuosity (with its alternating connotations of the heroic and the demonic) and of what I earlier referred to as the hegemony of the piano. And, as we saw in Chapter 1, part of the meaning of Liszt's Beethoven partitions lies in their reference to earlier transcriptions. Parodic transcriptions, such as Tatum's *Elegy*, also refer to preexisting meanings, but do so by way of undermining them.

Transcription differs from the five varieties of interpretation we distin-guished above. It differs from restoration, in that it does not presuppose an original that is to be restored. Because of this difference, successful tran-scription is not subject to the requirement that its processes reverse those whereby the object of interpretation arrived at its present state. Busoni's error was precisely to deny this difference. Transcription also differs from both explanation and restoration (where the object of interpretation *calls for* interpretation because it is lacking in a certain kind of manifest mean-ing). The object of transcription is not lacking in musical meaning. Tran-scription is not called for in that way; it is gratuitous.

Transcription differs from the activities of the preacher, and the director, in applying old texts to new contexts. In both these cases, as in transforma-tive transcription, interpretation amounts not to *finding* the object's mean-ing but to *making* it mean something new. But the transcriber's task is differ-ent from the preacher's in that the preacher may *state* the object's meaning, whereas the transcriber may not; it differs from the director's in that while both *show* the meaning, the transcriber does so by musical means and the director by theatrical means. Finally, transcription is different from criti-cism in that it does not issue in a statement about the object, but shows the object as having certain meanings.

Given the range of available representational techniques, it is clear that

11. Ibid., 453.
12. A homage need not be a transcription, as Davies reminds us ("Transcription, Authen-ticity, and Performance," 49).

there is always a range of treatments that could lead to a successful transcription. There is no one right transcription of a piece of music. This multiplism[13] is grounded in the fact that different meanings can convincingly be attached to different transcriptions of a single work, via different representations of it.

Do these transformations aim at truth? To a certain extent they do, because they seek to represent the object of interpretation, and in order to do so they must retain a certain amount of fidelity to that object. They achieve an *impression* of truth, too, in the meanings they impute to their respective objects. It is true that the *Die Meistersinger* Prelude is a contrapuntal work. Now, it is not true that the Bach Chaconne originated in an organ work—despite Busoni's beliefs to the contrary. The fact that this is not actually true does not detract from the transcription's success, however. The transcription succeeds because it allows us to understand Bach's original *as* a massive organ work. This is different from understanding *that* the original was such a work. Understanding-as, unlike understanding-that, does not involve a truth claim. Interpretation in general involves understanding-as, not understanding-that. It is only some particular species of interpretation that involve understanding-that.

Paraphrases, too, can be construed as interpretations. The menu of representational devices open to paraphrases is significantly wider than that available for nonparaphrasing transcriptions. Paraphrases may be much more selective in the way they represent their models, and they may reorder the model's contents. This is clear in Liszt's reminiscences of *Don Giovanni* (example 1.8). The music to be paraphrased, in this case, is a whole work (an opera) rather than a small part of it (an aria), and Liszt represents the opera through just two arias and a number of scattered phrases, reordered and recombined. A paraphrase's representation of its work may, therefore, be more abstract than the representation offered by a nonparaphrasing transcription. A successful nonparaphrasing transcription need not include representations of all the original work's features, but must include representations of all its temporal parts in their original order, without gaps or overlap. Successful paraphrases represent their parent works by selecting from among the temporal parts, allowing for gaps and overlaps between the representations of different temporal parts of the original.

13. Michael Krausz, *Rightness and Reasons: Interpretation in Cultural Practices* (Ithaca: Cornell University Press, 1993), 2.

How do we know what meaning the transcriber is assigning to the transcription? This can itself be a matter of interpretation. But we do not arrive randomly at such an interpretation. All transcribers, to the extent that they treat the music in some coherent fashion, aim to show the original music as possessing some type of meaning. Our interpretation can be checked against various data, such as the transcriber's other works, the historical context, and the transcriber's writings—especially those that accompany the transcription. Handel's style in his original keyboard works helps us understand the meaning of his keyboard transcriptions (example 1.5). The prefaces that accompany Liszt's, Busoni's, and Godowsky's transcriptions help us understand theirs.

It may seem that one can only call transcriptions interpretations in a derivative sense of "interpretation." Our construal of transcriptions as interpretations relies *inter alia* on the fact that transcriptions *delete* parts of the original music and *augment* the original work in various ways. But what the transcriber does, strictly speaking, is not to *execute* any actions of deletion or augmentation, but to *prescribe* certain performative actions that subtract from, or add to, the performative actions executed by someone playing the original work. So the transcriber's kind of activity is not, strictly speaking, the same as the interpreter's kind of activity, but it is conceptually derived from interpretation in the way that a prescription of an act is conceptually derived from the execution of that act. One cannot understand what it is to prescribe an act unless one understands what it is to execute that act, and so an understanding of a prescription is derivative upon an understanding of the act prescribed.

In considering this objection, we could take various things into account. First of all, we could say that even if it is true that transcriptions are interpretations only in a derivative sense, this would still place them closer to interpretations than Levinson allows when he says that it is merely a curious fact that musical interpretations go by that name. And even if transcriptions are only derivatively interpretations, it would still be important to understand the nature of the derivation. But we should also remember that even among nonperformative interpretations, we find similar relations of derivation. The critic *describes* what the archaeologist *executes;* critical interpretation, then, can be thought of as conceptually derivative upon the activity of the archaeologist in reconstructing a fragmentary artifact. We will return to the question of derivative and nonderivative senses of interpretation at the end of this chapter.

Variations

Some variations also fit our definition of interpretation, though not in the same way as transcriptions. Nelson Goodman states: "Variations upon a work, whether in the same or a different medium, and still more, sets of variations—are interpretations of the work."[14] I agree with his thesis in the case of those variations that are both experiential and aspectual. Certainly in all aspectual variations, the composer makes a representation of the theme in such a way that the variation's meanings are systematically related to those of the theme, within appropriate bounds of fidelity and creativity. The theme is the object of interpretation, and the composer is the interpreter. The variations are governed by a concern for creativity, while retaining enough continuity with the theme to allow for its representation, via what I have called the subject. But if the variation is not aspectual—if it does accord the theme a coherent treatment—then it lacks the kind of coherence that I assume is required in a successful interpretation. (I earlier suggested that the third variation of Beethoven's op. 111 [example 2.15] might lack the appropriate kind of coherence.)

If, on the other hand, the variation is not experiential—if we cannot hear the theme in it—then it cannot *show* the theme as having certain meanings, even though it might, in an abstract sense, have meaning-connections with the theme. (I suggested that Stravinsky's *Aldous Huxley In Memoriam* variations [examples 2.6 to 2.8] are not experiential representations of their theme.) In variations, difference is paramount, and community of meaning between variation and theme may have to be discovered through repeated listening or close analysis. As we discover these identities, the variation becomes an experiential one for us.

The identities in question do not have to be melodic; they may be harmonic. Classical works (with the exception of those involving figured bass) do not contain harmonic directives to performers. Rather, the harmony supervenes on other aspects of the music that are explicitly mandated. And yet, in the context of an individual variation, a theme may be represented exclusively by its harmony. We saw this in Byrd's Variation no. 9 on "The Woods So Wild" (example 2.12). The means whereby a variation represents its theme need not, then, include a selection of the theme's directives. In this respect, a variation differs from a transcription. A transcription cannot represent its model solely through harmonic means.

14. Goodman, "Variations on Variation," 82.

Amongst aspectual variations, we may apply our distinction between illumination and transformation, as we applied it to aspectual transcriptions. We noted Byrd's Variation no. 2 (example 2.11) as a case in which the theme is illuminated by a simple device. If the variation is experiential as well as aspectual (as this variation clearly is), then, because it represents the theme and shows it as having a certain meaning, it counts as an interpretation of that theme.

When Bach presents his theme in the guise of a French overture (example 2.4), or of other (named and unnamed) musical forms (example 2.16), he gives us so many transformative representations of his theme. In doing so, he makes musical meaning out of preexisting materials and thereby interprets his theme. The same is true of Beethoven's transformative representations of his theme (example 2.2). Some ways of transforming a theme show it in a negative light. Thus, if we follow Alfred Brendel's analysis, some of the Diabelli variations aim to ridicule the theme. Whether the transformation elevates or ridicules its theme, it functions as an interpretation of it.

Transformative variation differs from the five varieties of interpretation we mentioned earlier in the chapter. Variation does not aim to return to an origin; on the contrary, it aims to depart from one. Nor is it called for, if its object is to acquire meaning; on the contrary, the object already has musical meaning, and variation (like transcription) is gratuitous. Like transcription, variation *makes* musical meaning, rather than *discovering* it. Like transcription—and unlike the interpretive activity of the preacher or the critic—it *shows* this meaning. Like transcription, and unlike the interpretive activity of the director, it does so by musical means. Variation is also *unlike* transcription in various ways, as we showed in Chapter 2.

There is always more than one way of varying a theme. It would be nonsensical for someone to ask what the right variation on a given theme might be. Different aspects of the theme may be chosen as subjects for different variations, and each subject is open to a variety of treatments. Variations (despite the claims of Donald Tovey and Edward Said) do not aim to disclose what is secreted in the theme. They are not interpretations of the truth-seeking variety. The composer of variations does not aim to discover what is present in the theme, but invents musical meanings around a representation of the theme. This is the playful activity of a creative artist, not the authoritative probing of the philologist. Of course, a variation, like a transcription, has to get some aspects of the theme right: these are the aspects that it appropriates as its subject. But that is not to say that it must get the theme as a whole right. Frequently, the variation has the constructive aim of absorbing its subject in a new musical context, just as the object of a constructive interpretation is made part of a larger whole and given a new meaning.

Realizations

The question of whether realizations may be interpretations reduces to the question of whether executive realizations may be interpretations. This is because notational realizations are, in effect, plans to execute musical works. They will therefore have the character of interpretations to the extent that performances do.

Executive realizations may be interpretations. This statement would come as no surprise to critics and musicians, who commonly assume that executive realization (at least in the hands of a performer who is an artist) is interpretation. They are not among the "we" who, according to Levinson, appear to think of interpretation primarily as critical interpretation. Here, for instance, is Walter Frei writing about Wilhelm Backhaus: "the score is only a partial representation of the work: it needs the element of sound, and calls for an interpreter, a 'go-between' and translator, who will thus transform it. It was to this enabling task that Backhaus dedicated himself."[15] And here is Vladimir Horowitz on himself: "The printed score is important, but the interpretation of it has been the object of my life study."[16]

To musicians and lovers of music, it may indeed be obvious that executive realization is interpretation, but that does not exonerate us from providing a philosophical argument in support of this thesis. It would suffice for us to show that such realization is structured in the way interpretation is: an interpreter makes a representation of the object of interpretation, which states or shows the object's meaning, under constraints of fidelity and creativity. If this can be shown, then clearly it is not just a curious fact that realizations are called interpretations. On the contrary, they will be seen as fitting our broad concept of interpretation. On that basis it will be reasonable to agree with Richard Wollheim, who argues that there is "a strict parallel" between performative interpretation and critical interpretation.[17]

15. Walter Frei, liner notes to *Beethoven, Piano Sonatas 1–32*, perf. Wilhelm Backhaus, Decca 433 882 2, 10.

16. Vladimir Horowitz quoted in Elyse Mach, ed., *Great Contemporary Pianists Speak for Themselves* (New York: Dover, 1988), 116.

17. Richard Wollheim, *Art and Its Objects*, 2nd ed. (Cambridge: Cambridge University Press, 1980), 84–85.

Wollheim also asserts that because performative interpretation "may be regarded as the production of a token that has properties in excess of those of the type," it follows that "every performance of a work involves, or is, an interpretation."[18] It turns out, however, that our broad concept of interpretation supports this conclusion only in a qualified sense.

An executive realization of a musical work is a sequence of actions performed in compliance with the work's instructions. Such a realization, like the interpretation of an object, involves representation. In this case, a sequence of actions represents a work. This representation may have been arrived at by processes such as cutting repeats or whole sections of the work, or altering the requirements indicated in the score (for example, by adding ornamentation or cadenzas)—processes that are essentially akin to those used in transcription and variation. But some types of representation occur in those forms of composition and do not occur in realization. Abstraction, for example, while common in variation form, is not a mode of representation that occurs in realization (which, on the contrary, makes its object more concrete). Equally, there are certain means of representation that are open to performers in realizing a work but are not open to the composer of transcriptions or variations. Performers can place an individual stamp on the music through their personal physical qualities—qualities that may be typified by what Roland Barthes called "the grain of the voice."[19]

We need to distinguish among musical realizations as we did among transcriptions and variations—those that are experiential and those that are aspectual representations. We noted in Chapter 3 that a performance (as opposed to a mere playing) represents its work experientially, and that a work that is executed in such a way that it cannot be recognized is played but not performed.

Must a performance represent its work aspectually? In a sense, the answer has to be negative when the music is played in a routine manner that does no more than the minimum required to execute and project the score's instructions. Relative to the content of those instructions, nothing new is produced in a routine performance. Equally, when a performer (such as Horowitz in his less successful performances) plays in an incoherent manner that fails to apply any global treatment to the music—even if it applies several local treatments to different sections—the performance fails to represent the music aspectually. Because a nonaspectual representation must

18. Ibid., 98, 99.
19. Barthes, "The Grain of the Voice," 181ff.

fail to be an interpretation, I cannot agree with Wollheim's statement that all performance involves interpretation.

In another sense, though, even a routine or incoherent performance produces meaning simply by virtue of the fact that a human agent executes and projects the work, thereby instantiating some, at least, of the work's meanings. We could describe this minimal level of aspectual representation by saying that even in a routine performance, the work is made flesh. A performance always produces meaning at least in this minimal sense, and, as even a routine or incoherent performance shows its object as possessing meaning in this way, we can conclude that even such performances count as interpretations of the work performed.

But when a performance is coherent, it shows the meaning of the music in a more full-blooded way. Such are the performances that Franz Liszt had in mind when writing about the pianist's duty to bring *life* to the music:

> He is called upon to make emotion speak, and weep, and sing, and sigh—to bring it to life in his consciousness. He creates as the composer himself created, for he himself must live the passions he will call to light in all their brilliance. He breathes life into the lethargic body, infuses it with fire, enlivens it with the pulse of grace and charm. He changes the earthy form into a living being, penetrating it with the spark which Prometheus snatched from Jupiter's flesh. He must send the form he has created soaring into transparent ether; he must arm it with a thousand winged weapons; he must call up scent and blossom, and breathe the breath of life.[20]

Here we have a rich field of metaphorical meaning. The Lisztian performer is the agent who gives life to the otherwise "earthy form" of the work, and through the reference to Prometheus this life is portrayed as having a divine source. The idea of life is a highly charged one, and to think of performance as bestowing life on a work is to think of it as endowing the work with meaning in a robust sense.

Individual performances are frequently thought of as not simply enlivening the work performed but also giving it a specific type of life. For example, Wilhelm Backhaus's piano playing has been described as displaying "a wonderfully muscular animality in which a superb life force is at work."[21]

20. Reginald R. Gerig, *Great Pianists and Their Technique* (Washington: R. B. Luce, c. 1974), 193–94. Quoted in Sachs, *Virtuoso*, 61.

21. David Dubal, liner notes to *Grand Piano: Brahms,* with Harold Bauer, Wilhelm Backhaus, Edwin Fischer, Carl Friedberg, Myra Hess, and Arthur Rubinstein, Nimbus NI 8806.

Vladimir Horowitz's Scarlatti has been described as possessing a "feline grace,"[22] while his playing of the Chopin Mazurkas has been thought of as effecting a "reconciliation of peasant vitality and aristocratic refinement."[23] These metaphors of realization as bestowing particular forms of life on the work carry with them specific attributions of musical meaning. To that extent, they impute specific musical interpretations to the performing artist.

Sometimes, when a realization produces musical meaning, it shows the work being performed as possessing that meaning. It illuminates the work. In Chapter 3, we considered authenticist and objectivist realizations, along with Lang Lang's performance of the Liszt *Don Giovanni* paraphrase, in this light. Moreover, a realization sometimes transforms the work, as, for example, Presley's realization of "Hound Dog" does. And sometimes a realization undermines or ridicules the work being performed. We considered Gould's *Appassionata* Sonata in this way. In all these cases, by virtue of their production of musical meaning, such realizations must count as interpretations of the music performed.

David Saltz reminds us that, in the case of dramatic performances, most of the properties by which a performance exceeds the work performed are irrelevant to any interpretation that the performance may contain.[24] For example, the actor playing Juliet may be taller than the one playing Romeo, but this fact may have no bearing on the interpretation of the play. Saltz thinks that this shows that performances are not interpretations at all. But that conclusion does not follow. Fido is a dog, but that does not mean that all of Fido's features form part of his being a dog: many, such as his spatial location or his being my current pet, do not. So even if most of a realization's features are not part of any interpretation, the realization may still be an interpretation of its topic work.

At this point, it is worth asking whether a realization is ever an implementation of a critical interpretation of a musical work. In Chapter 3 we noted Alfred Cortot's critical interpretation of Chopin's *Funeral March* Sonata as a poem of death and his understanding of the last movement as depicting the wind howling over gravestones. We also noted his view that this understanding of the last movement could be conveyed in performance by adding a sudden *crescendo* to Chopin's score—and we saw that he actually executed this *crescendo* in his 1933 recording. Should we count a performance that

22. Max Harrison, liner notes to *Vladimir Horowitz Recordings, 1930–1951*, EMI, CHS 7 63538 2, 8.
23. Ibid.
24. Saltz, "What Theatrical Performance Is (Not)," 301.

executes that *crescendo* as implementing his literary interpretation of the movement? It hardly seems necessary. A pianist might not be aware of the literary interpretation and might play the *crescendo* for a variety of reasons.

At the same time, it must be admitted that sometimes a given performative interpretation fits better with a given critical interpretation than other performative interpretations do. The dynamic effect recommended by Cortot, for instance, would be an *appropriate* device for a pianist who wanted to implement his literary interpretation of the Finale, in the sense that a listener familiar with the wind-over-gravestones interpretation could hear this sudden *crescendo* as enhancing the prevailing atmosphere of "sinister, repressed excitement."[25] At the same time, it would not be correct to say simply that a performance following Cortot's recommendations *embodies* his literary interpretation. Even if the performer thinks of the literary interpretation while playing, those thoughts may not actually be projected by the performance. What is true is that given a context that includes familiarity with the literary interpretation, a listener might well make sense of the *crescendo* as fitting into that interpretation. Other interpretive contexts might lead to the same outcome: for instance, a listener familiar with similarly constructed film music illustrating ghoulish graveyard scenes might well come to hear the whole movement as wind over the tombstones. Also helpful would be a familiarity with various factors surrounding the performance, such as interviews with the pianist and program notes (to the extent that these reflect the pianist's views). These interpretive contexts would be helpful to the listener in much the same way as titles and catalogues are helpful to the interpreter of visual art. At the same time, it has to be admitted that a listener unable to draw upon any such context may well hear the sudden *crescendo* simply as a puzzling disruption. What can be said in general is that, while performances do not objectively embody critical interpretations, still, given a suitable interpretive context, a listener can hear a performance as embodying a particular interpretation. If we imaginatively isolate the listener from all interpretive contexts, though, then we remove all such possibilities of hearing-as. In this sense, it is legitimate to apply the term "interpretation" to performances—but relative to particular interpretive contexts. Yet to speak in this way of a performance is not to report a fact about the performance, but to interpret it. The listener is the interpreter, and according to the listener's interpretation, the performance implements a certain critical interpretation of the work.

25. Rosen, *The Romantic Generation*, 300.

This, then, is one way in which a realization can be—or can be interpreted as—an interpretation of a musical work. But it is not the only way. Not all performative interpretations are implementations of critical interpretations. In many instances, the performance *shows* something about the work—something that could not fully be said, and therefore could not be fully expressed in a critical interpretation.

Conclusion

In this final chapter I have outlined a concept of interpretation as an activity that finds meaning in an object or imputes meaning to an object. This activity is characteristically subject to potentially conflicting requirements of fidelity and creativity, requirements that it attempts to meet by a dual process of representation and treatment. I have argued that some transcriptions, variations, and realizations fit this concept of interpretation—not unconditionally, but subject to the condition that they state or show a coherent meaning, and in the case of performances, that they successfully project this meaning. Relative to this concept of interpretation, it turns out that composers and performers are sometimes interpreters, and that musical works and performances are sometimes interpretations. Critical interpretations and performative interpretations both fall under this concept, and to that extent it is no mere accident that there is interpretation of both types.

The different types of musical interpretation exhibit analogies with one another. These analogies indicate a shared structure and teleology. There is an object of interpretation, whether it be a theme or a work. There is a process of representation, and whether this be by operations of deletion, augmentation, distortion, or reordering, the product of these operations is something that has the same function in all cases (namely, to state or show a meaning as belonging to the object). There is a treatment, and this is what someone understands when he or she understands the transcription, the variation, or the realization as what it is. And there is the basic challenge facing any interpreter (at least, any interpreter who would be an artist), namely, to find a way of balancing fidelity with creativity.

The ascription of musical meaning to transcriptions, variations, and realizations entails that they invite particular types of musical understanding, that is, particular ways of hearing-as. The shared purpose of all these arts—the art of transcription, that of variation, and that of realization—is to make musical meaning, but different things count as musical meaning in each art.

A transcription gives its parent work a new voice. A variation transforms its theme. A realization takes the relatively abstract entity that is the musical work and makes it concrete. These are all, potentially, ways of making musical meaning. The constraints of fidelity and creativity are common, but they are assigned different weights in the three types of musical interpretation. A transcription faithfully reproduces certain of the work's features, while a variation may choose to vary precisely those features. In a realization, performers are caught up in a dialectic that invites them to display themselves as creative artists while calling on them to respect the work they claim to be realizing.

There are always multiple ways of playing out this dialectic. There is always more than one way of writing an artistic transcription of a musical work while maintaining an appropriate level of fidelity to the work. There is always more than one way to vary a theme without losing it. There is always more than one way of realizing a piece while still executing the piece's directives.

Artists as diverse as Vladimir Horowitz and Claudio Arrau avow this plurality of realizations. Horowitz emphasizes the need for the pianist to "do something" with the music:

> You have to open the music, so to speak, and see what's behind the notes because the notes are the same whether it is the music of Bach or someone else. But behind the notes something different is told and that's what the interpreter must find out. He may sit down and play one passage one way and then perhaps exaggerate the next, but, in any event, he must do something with the music. The worst thing is not to do anything. It may even be something you don't like, but do it! The printed score is important, but the interpretation of it has been the object of my life study.[26]

And, of course, different musicians will "do" different things—as will Horowitz himself on different occasions. Arrau places much more emphasis on fidelity to the score, but he also holds that the pianist must "build a vision" of his own:

> If the composer noted that a passage should be played *fortissimo,* then it should be played *fortissimo,* not *pianissimo.* On the other hand, this fidelity and loyalty to what the composer wanted is only a basis on which the artist builds his own vision, his own idea

26. Vladimir Horowitz, in *Great Contemporary Pianists,* ed. Mach, 116.

of the work. But the vision must not jeopardize his respect for the text, or what he might know about the intentions of the composer. Some pianists "use" the original music and change it into a form of self-expression only. This is wrong. Others seem to be so awed by the composer that they do the opposite: They play nothing *but* the notes. This is wrong too. A good artist goes into a flight of imagination on his own, but he never destroys the integrity of the work as the composer saw it.[27]

The pluralism that these artists find in performative interpretation is also to be found in critical interpretations, if by a critical interpretation we understand a view of a work, possibly partial, that potentially competes with rival views of the same work. Like the performing artist, the critic who is engaged in crafting such an interpretation highlights certain features of the object at the expense of others. Some of the object's features may be put aside as not relevant to critical evaluation, because they are regarded as imperfections in the work or because they do not bear on the particular kind of interpretation being attempted. Material that falls outside the object of interpretation may be brought into play for interpretive purposes. Because such representations clearly admit of alternative constructions, critical interpretations in this sense are inherently plural.

Levinson favors a sense of "critical interpretation" according to which critical interpretation is not open to this pluralism because it aims at comprehensively integrating the differing partially valid or narrowly legitimate interpretations into a single synthesis: "I suggest that it is always possible, in principle, to combine competing reasonable first-order interpretations of a work so as to embrace them as a totality from a more encompassing perspective."[28] But this, to my mind, is a *second-order* sense of interpretation. In the *first-order* sense, critical interpretations characteristically do possess what Torsten Pettersson calls "pliability," namely, "a combination of flexibility and resistance."[29] So I think that we can continue to maintain, *pace* Levinson, that first-order critical interpretations take their place alongside performative realizations as both inherently plural.

27. Claudio Arrau, in ibid., 4.

28. Jerrold Levinson, "Hypothetical Intentionalism: Statement, Objections, and Replies," in *Is There a Single Right Interpretation?* ed. Michael Krausz (University Park: The Pennsylvania State University Press, 2002), 310.

29. Torsten Pettersson, "Literary Work as a Pliable Entity: Combining Realism with Pluralism," in *Is There a Single Right Interpretation?* ed. Krausz, 219–20, 223.

Bibliography

Apel, Willi. *A History of Keyboard Music to 1700.* Translated and revised by Hans Tischler. Bloomington: Indiana University Press, 1972.

Barber, Nicholas. "Hound Dog." In *Lives of the Great Songs: The Greatest Pop Song Stories Collection—Ever!* edited by Tim De Lisle, 202–7. London: Penguin Books, 1994.

Barthes, Roland. "The Grain of the Voice." In *Image-Music-Text: Essays Selected and Translated by Stephen Heath,* 183–85. London: Fontana, 1977.

———. "Musica Practica." In *Image-Music-Text: Essays Selected and Translated by Stephen Heath,* 149–54. London: Fontana, 1977.

Brendel, Alfred. "Beethoven's Diabelli Variations." In *On Music: Collected Essays,* 113–27. Chicago: A Cappella, 2001.

———. "Form and Psychology in Beethoven's Piano Sonatas." In *On Music: Collected Essays,* 42–57. Chicago: A Cappella, 2001.

———. "Liszt's Piano Playing." In *On Music: Collected Essays,* 279–81. Chicago: A Cappella, 2001.

———. "Turning the Piano into an Orchestra." In *On Music: Collected Essays,* 282–87. Chicago: A Cappella, 2001.

Budd, Malcolm. *Values of Art: Pictures, Poetry, and Music.* London: Penguin Books, 1995.

Busoni, Ferruccio. *Sketch of a New Esthetic of Music.* Translated by Theodore Baker. New York: G. Schirmer, 1911. [Reprinted in *Three Classics in the Aesthetic of Music* (New York: Dover, 1962).]

———. *Toccata and Fugue in D Minor, and Other Bach Transcriptions for Solo Piano.* New York: Dover, 1966.

Caldwell, John. *English Keyboard Music Before the Nineteenth Century.* Oxford: Blackwell, 1973.

Cooper, Martin. "Massenet." In *The New Grove Dictionary of Music and Musicians,* edited by Stanley Sadie, 11:801. London: Macmillan, 1980.

Cortot, Alfred, ed. *Édition de travail des oeuvres de Chopin: Scherzos.* Paris: Éditions Salabert, 1933.

———. *Édition de travail des oeuvres de Chopin: Sonate Op. 35.* Paris: Éditions Salabert, 1930.

Daintith, John, and R. D. Nelson. *The Penguin Dictionary of Mathematics*. London: Penguin Books, 1989.

Danto, Arthur. *The Transfiguration of the Commonplace: A Philosophy of Art*. Cambridge, Mass.: Harvard University Press, 1981.

Davies, Stephen. "Authenticity in Musical Performance." In *Themes in the Philosophy of Music*, 81–93. Oxford: Oxford University Press, 2003.

———. *Musical Meaning and Expression*. Ithaca: Cornell University Press, 1994.

———. *Musical Works and Performances: A Philosophical Exploration*. Oxford: Clarendon Press, 2001.

———. "The Ontology of Musical Works and the Authenticity of Their Performances." In *Themes in the Philosophy of Music*, 60–77. Oxford: Oxford University Press, 2003.

———. *Themes in the Philosophy of Music*. Oxford: Oxford University Press, 2003.

———. "Transcription, Authenticity, and Performance." In *Themes in the Philosophy of Music*, 47–59. Oxford: Oxford University Press, 2003.

Dubal, David. Liner notes to *Grand Piano: Brahms*. With Harold Bauer, Wilhelm Backhaus, Edwin Fischer, Carl Friedberg, Myra Hess, and Artur Rubinstein. Nimbus NI 8806.

Elgin, Catherine Z. "Goodman, Nelson." In *A Companion to Aesthetics*, edited by David E. Cooper, 175–77. Oxford: Blackwell, 1992.

Frei, Walter. Liner notes to *Beethoven, Piano Sonatas 1–32*. Wilhelm Backhaus. Decca 433 882 2.

Goodman, Nelson. "Variations on Variation—or Picasso Back to Bach." In *Reconceptions in Philosophy and Other Arts and Sciences*, by Nelson Goodman and Catherine Z. Elgin, 66–82. London: Routledge, 1988.

Grout, Donald J. *A History of Western Music*. New York: W. W. Norton, 1973.

Handel, George Frideric. *Handel's Sixty Overtures from All His Operas and Oratorios Set for the Harpsicord or Organ*. London: I. Walsh, n.d. [Reprinted as George Frideric Handel, *60 Handel Overtures Arranged for Solo Keyboard* (New York: Dover, 1993).]

———. *Twenty Overtures in Authentic Keyboard Arrangements*. Edited by Terence Best. 3 vols. London: Novello, 1985–86.

Harrison, Max. Liner notes to *Vladimir Horowitz Recordings, 1930–1951*. EMI CHS 7 63538 2.

Hopkins, Charles. Liner notes to *Bach-Busoni Transcriptions—2*. Nikolai Demidenko. Hyperion CDA 67324.

Horowitz, Joseph. *Arrau on Music and Performance*. Mineola, N.Y.: Dover, 1999.

Howard, Joseph A. "The Improvisational Techniques of Art Tatum." 2 vols. Ph.D. diss., Case Western Reserve University, 1978.

Kivy, Peter. *Authenticities: Philosophical Reflections on Musical Performance*. Ithaca: Cornell University Press, 1995.

Kramer, Lawrence. *Musical Meaning: Toward a Critical History*. Berkeley and Los Angeles: University of California Press, 2002.

Krausz, Michael. *Rightness and Reasons: Interpretation in Cultural Practices*. Ithaca: Cornell University Press, 1993.

————, ed. *Is There a Single Right Interpretation?* (University Park: The Pennsylvania State University Press, 2002).

Levinson, Jerrold. "Hypothetical Intentionalism: Statement, Objections, and Replies." In *Is There a Single Right Interpretation?* edited by Michael Krausz, 309–18. University Park: The Pennsylvania State University Press, 2002.

————. *Music in the Moment.* Ithaca: Cornell University Press, 1997.

————. "Performative vs. Critical Interpretation in Music." In *The Interpretation of Music,* edited by Michael Krausz, 33–60. Oxford: Clarendon Press, 1993.

Liszt, Franz. *Beethoven Symphonies Nos. 1–5 Transcribed for Solo Piano.* Mineola, N.Y.: Dover, 1998.

Macdonald, Hugh. Liner notes to *Symphonie Fantastique,* by Hector Berlioz. The London Classical Players. Roger Norrington. EMI CDC 7 49541 2.

Mach, Elyse, ed. *Great Contemporary Pianists Speak for Themselves.* New York: Dover, 1988.

Mann, Thomas. *Doctor Faustus: The Life of the German Composer Adrian Leverkühn as Told by a Friend.* Translated by H. T. Lowe-Porter. New York: Penguin Books, 1968.

Massenet, Jules. *Élégie.* London: Edwin Ashdown; Sydney: D. Davis, c. 1890.

Mautner, Thomas, ed. *The Penguin Dictionary of Philosophy.* Rev. ed. London: Penguin Books, 2000.

Miller, Jonathan. *Subsequent Performances.* London: Faber and Faber, 1986.

Moroney, Davitt. Liner notes to *William Byrd: The Complete Keyboard Music.* Davitt Moroney. Hyperion CDA 66551/7 (7 compact discs).

Orga, Ateş, and Nikolai Demidenko. Liner notes to *Bach-Busoni Transcriptions.* Nikolai Demidenko. Hyperion CDA 66566.

Payzant, Geoffrey. *Glenn Gould: Music and Mind.* Toronto: Key Porter Books, 1984.

Pettersson, Torsten. "The Literary Work as a Pliable Entity: Combining Realism with Pluralism." In *Is There a Single Right Interpretation?* edited by Michael Krausz, 211–30. University Park: The Pennsylvania State University Press, 2002.

Peyser, Joan. *To Boulez and Beyond: Music in Europe Since "The Rite of Spring."* New York: Billboard Books, 1999.

Phillips, Peter. Liner notes to *Josquin: L'homme armé Masses.* The Tallis Scholars. Peter Phillips. Gimell CDGIM 019.

Priestley, Brian. "Ragtime, Blues, Jazz, and Popular Music." In *The Cambridge Companion to the Piano,* edited by David Rowland, 209–24. Cambridge: Cambridge University Press, 1998.

Rose, Margaret. *Parody: Ancient, Modern, and Post-Modern.* Cambridge: Cambridge University Press, 1993.

Rosen, Charles. *The Classical Style: Haydn, Mozart, Beethoven.* London: Faber and Faber, 1971.

————. *The Romantic Generation.* London: Fontana, 1999.

Roy, Samuel. *Elvis: Prophet of Power.* Brookline, Mass.: Branden, 1985.

Sachs, Harvey. *Virtuoso: The Life and Art of Niccolò Paganini, Franz Liszt, Anton Rubinstein, Ignace Jan Paderewski, Fritz Kreisler, Pablo Casals, Wanda*

Landowska, Vladimir Horowitz, Glenn Gould. London: Thames and Hudson, 1982.

Said, Edward. *Musical Elaborations.* London: Vintage, 1992.

Saltz, David. "What Theatrical Performance Is (Not): The Interpretation Fallacy." *Journal of Aesthetics and Art Criticism* 59 (2001): 299–306.

Schonberg, Harold C. *The Great Pianists.* New York: Simon and Schuster, 1963.

———. *Horowitz: His Life and Music.* London: Simon and Schuster, 1992.

Schuller, Gunther. *The Swing Era: The Development of Jazz, 1930–1945.* New York: Oxford University Press, 1989.

Scruton, Roger. *The Aesthetics of Music.* Oxford: Clarendon Press, 1997.

———. "Wittgenstein and the Understanding of Music." *The British Journal of Aesthetics* 44 (2004): 1–9.

Searle, John R., and Daniel Vanderveken. *Foundations of Illocutionary Logic.* Cambridge: Cambridge University Press, 1985.

Sontag, Susan. *Against Interpretation and Other Essays.* New York: Delta, 1961.

Stegemann, Michael. Liner notes to *Beethoven Piano Sonatas, Vol. 2.* Glenn Gould. Sony SM3K 52642 (3 compact discs).

———. Liner notes to *The Glenn Gould Edition: Wagner, Siegfried-Idyll, Wagner-Gould, Die Meistersinger von Nürnberg, Götterdämmerung, Siegfried-Idyll Piano Transcriptions.* Glenn Gould. Sony SMK 52650.

Steinberg, Michael. Liner notes to *Stravinsky in America.* London Symphony Orchestra. Michael Tilson Thomas. RCA 09026-668865-2.

Tatum, Art. *Art Tatum: Jazz Masters.* Arranged by Jed Distler. New York: Amsco, 1986.

———. *Elegy.* Transcribed by Jed Distler. *Keyboard Classics and Piano Stylist* (November/December 1994): 36–38.

Thom, Paul. *For an Audience: A Philosophy of the Performing Arts.* Philadelphia: Temple University Press, 1993.

———. *Making Sense: A Theory of Interpretation.* Lanham, Md.: Rowman and Littlefield, 2000.

———. "On Changing the Subject." *Metaphilosophy* 31 (2001): 63–74.

von Fischer, Kurt. "Variations." In *The New Grove Dictionary of Music and Musicians,* edited by Stanley Sadie, 19:537. London: Macmillan, 1980.

White, Eric Walter. *Stravinsky: The Composer and His Works.* 2nd ed. Berkeley and Los Angeles: University of California Press, 1979.

Wollheim, Richard. *Art and Its Objects.* 2nd ed. Cambridge: Cambridge University Press, 1980.

Recordings

Bach, Johann Sebastian, and Anton Webern. *Ricercar.* Münchener Kammerorchester, The Hilliard Ensemble. Christoph Poppen. ECM New Series 1744 B0000048-02.

Byrd, William. *William Byrd: The Complete Keyboard Music.* Davitt Moroney. Hyperion CDA 66551/7 (7 compact discs).

Cortot, Alfred, perf. *Chopin: Piano Concerto No. 2, Sonatas 2 and 3.* Allegro CDO 3037.

Gibbons, Orlando. *Masters of Early English Keyboard Music IV: Orlando Gibbons and Giles Farnaby.* Thurston Dart. Éditions de l'oiseau-lyre OL 50131.

Gould, Glenn, perf. *Beethoven Piano Sonatas, Vol. 2.* Sony SM3K 52642 (3 compact discs).

———, perf. *The Glenn Gould Edition: Wagner, Siegfried-Idyll, Wagner-Gould, Die Meistersinger von Nürnberg, Götterdämmerung, Siegfried-Idyll Piano Transcriptions.* Sony SMK 52650.

Hewitt, Angela, perf. *Johann Sebastian Bach, Goldberg Variations: Aria mit verschiedenen Veränderungen ("Aria with Diverse Variations"), BWV988.* Hyperion CDA 67305.

Hofmann, Josef, perf. *Grand Piano: Josef Hofmann.* Nimbus NI 8803.

———. *Great Pianists of the 20th Century: Josef Hofmann.* Philips 456 835-2.

Lang, Lang, perf. *Lang Lang Live at Carnegie Hall: Schumann, Haydn, Schubert, Tan Dun, Chopin, Liszt.* Deutsche Grammophon DJ-503.

Leschetitzsky, Theodor, perf. *Nocturne in D Flat Major Op. 27 No. 2, by Frédéric Chopin. Berühmte Pianisten um die Jahrhundertwende.* Telefunken HT 32.

Presley, Elvis, perf. *Presley: The All-Time Greatest Hits.* RCA ND 9000.

Tatum, Art, perf. *The Definitive Art Tatum.* Blue Note 7243 5 40225 2 4.

Thornton, Willie Mae, perf. *Big Mama Thornton: The Original Hound Dog.* Peacock Ace CDCHD 940.

Thomas, Michael Tilson, cond. *Stravinsky in America.* London Symphony Orchestra. RCA 09026-68865-2.

Zeisler, Fannie Bloomfield, perf. *Fannie Bloomfield Zeisler, 1863-1927.* Pierian 0003/4.

Index